A CHOICE
OF WORLDS

UNDER THE ADVISORY EDITORSHIP OF

J. Jeffery Auer

A CHOICE
OF WORLDS

THE PRACTICE AND CRITICISM
OF PUBLIC DISCOURSE

James R. Andrews
INDIANA UNIVERSITY

Harper & Row, Publishers

NEW YORK   EVANSTON

SAN FRANCISCO   LONDON

For Moya

Contents

Preface

The underlying assumption of this book is that the student of public address is both a producer and a consumer; the principles of rhetoric are studied for their usefulness to the speaker and critic alike. The principles discussed in Part One are not, obviously, new. They are simply my distillation and synthesis of basic ideas that have been examined and refined over centuries by scholarly investigation and speculation. What is of prime importance to the student is the awareness that concepts of rhetorical effectiveness need not *only* help him to prepare a good speech; they are equally useful to him as he attempts to sort out and evaluate the mass of communication events to which he is exposed daily. Accordingly, this book, in its effort to help students develop a rhetorical perspective, explains principles, relates them to the needs of the speaker and the critic, and offers examples of how they may be used in specific critical situations.

The critical introductions, it is emphasized, are *examples, not models,* of criticism. Different critics, applying the same principles, might reach different conclusions and produce different critical insights. Far from being the final word about the speeches examined, the critical introductions should provide a starting point for discussion about the critical process. Each critical essay attempts to show how each principle might be used to provide a way for the critic to approach a speech. It certainly will be recognized that the factors discussed in any given speech are not the only ones that could be investigated.

The primary source for the criticisms are the speeches themselves. While it would be impossible to understand the rhetorical power of a speech outside of the historical context in which it was given, and while a critic could not function without a knowledge of the audience and occasion for the speech, the historical background is, after all, subsidiary to the critic's investigation of the actual message. It is for this reason that the critical introductions focus most sharply on the speech texts.

The speeches chosen deal with issues of universal importance. They are both contemporary and historical. They may, hopefully, demonstrate that relevance is not the same as immediacy, and that understanding the impact of basic ideas and evaluating the flow of never-ending communication may well rest, in part, on the development of an historical perspective within the rhetorical perspective.

There are, of course, many who have helped me in a variety of ways in preparing this work, and it is impossible to acknowledge them all. I am especially grateful to my wife. Not only has she created a climate in which it was possible for me to work, she also has helped in a myriad of ways on the manuscript itself; her perceptive and tactful critical suggestions never failed to cause me to see problems and state conclusions more clearly. Inevitably, a book of this sort is ultimately the result of the author's contact with the work of many others and with teachers, students, and colleagues. Though none of them can be blamed for the faults of the output, I am certainly grateful to them for the input over the years.

James R. Andrews

Bloomington, Indiana

PART ONE:

The Rhetoric
of Public
Discourse

1

Introduction:
The Study
of Public Discourse

A student broadside circulated to members of the Columbia University community attempted to distinguish between the liberal and radical positions. In defense against a charge of quibbling over words, the students replied simply, eloquently, and perceptively: "A choice of words is a choice of worlds."

Men have always attempted to portray their world—the world as it is, and the world as it ought to be—through words. The public utterances of social and political leaders can form the highest expressions of the aspirations of the groups for whom and to whom they speak. When William Pitt told the eighteenth-century House of Commons that "Americans are the sons and not the bastards of England" he put forcefully and strikingly into words the concept that men in a political society that calls itself "free" must offer equality of opportunity and participation—a concept not so very different from Martin Luther King's "dream."

Through public speaking, a society's values and goals are refined and articulated. A study of the speeches of the past gives strong indications of the roots of our national ideals; contemporary speeches illustrate the ways in which modern man thinks about and attempts to deal with his political, social, and moral heritage. There can be little doubt that past rhetorical efforts have succeeded in setting standards for our nation. The current American crises, the crises on the campuses, in the cities, and in our relations with other nations and peoples, are certainly in part traceable to the difficulty which the American culture has had in turning abstract ideals into concrete realities. If America is undergoing a new revolution, it is in some ways a reflection of the revolution that established this nation. One student of contemporary public discourse, for example, has thoughtfully and perceptively examined the rhetoric of Black Power. Parke G. Burgess observes that "Beneath the call to arms may be a cry for justice and community, as beneath the anger may be disappointment and disillusion." [1] Blacks, students, antiwar demonstrators consistently hark back to what they consider fundamental American principles of equality and justice, articulated at our eighteenth-century birth. The rhetorical effectiveness of our heritage is strongly attested by the values we profess in this century. John F. Kennedy reminded Americans that "We dare not forget today that we are the heirs of that first revolution." When President Kennedy in his Inaugural Address described the revolutionary belief to which the country was still committed as "the belief that the rights of man come not from the generosity of the state, but from the hand of God," [2] he stood in direct rhetorical descent from such early spokesman as Thomas Paine who stood for "the natural rights of all mankind," and who wrote in *Common Sense* of "the Cause of America," which was "the cause of all mankind." [3] The ideals of the Revolution are still the rallying cry of those who would change our modern society. So, then, what has been argued and advanced in the past has a decided impact on and relevance for what we do and say in the present.

While man can use public speaking to inspire, to move, to articulate the aims of his society, he can also use the public platform to deceive, to destroy, to exploit the goals of his hearers. He can appeal to "the better angels of our nature," or play upon our most twisted fears and insecurities. All of us know that we do not always do what is best for us; we often do what we want to do, not what we perhaps ought to do. Furthermore, we many times have no real idea

[1] Parke G. Burgess, "The Rhetoric of Black Power: A Moral Demand?" in J. Jeffery Auer, ed., *The Rhetoric of Our Times*, New York: Appleton, 1969, p. 61.

[2] John F. Kennedy, "Inaugural Address," in Robert T. Oliver and Eugene E. White, eds., *Selected Speeches from American History*, Boston: Allyn & Bacon, 1966, pp. 284–285.

[3] Thomas Paine, Introduction to "Common Sense," in Harry Hayden Clark, ed., *Representative Selections*, rev. ed., American Century Series, New York: Hill & Wang, 1961, p. 3.

of *what* we ought to do. There is a strong, human temptation to ease the tension, to give up the struggle to react *critically* to communication. Bombarded as we are by messages competing for our attention and adherence, we need to develop as our defense not so much a long list of "rules" to judge the goodness or badness of appeals, but, rather, a *rhetorical perspective* from which we can sort out and evaluate the verbal avalanche. Failure of a people to react critically to persuasion has, in the past, had disastrous consequences. From the witch hunts of Salem to the pogroms of Nazi Germany men have allowed their frustrations, envies, guilts, and fears to be focused outside of themselves, to be drained off through simplistic, destructive solutions to deep and subtle problems. America has had and still has extremists of all varieties who would short-circuit the critical stance and fix upon a scapegoat the blame for all ills. It is obvious that those who would burn a cross to intimidate or plant a bomb to annihilate pose a grave threat to the operation of the persuasive process. But those of us who categorically accept, reject, or ignore messages without filtering them through a rhetorically critical screen, are likewise dangerous people—to ourselves and others. For what we do or fail to do as a result of what we hear can directly affect our health, our lives, and the lives of others—and will undoubtedly shape the quality of life in this country and in the world. Those who would direct us down destructive, antihumanistic paths must be carefully studied. When the great modern critic Kenneth Burke wrote of "The Rhetoric of Hitler's 'Battle' " he implored thoughtful men to try to "discover what kind of 'medicine' this medicine-man has concocted, that we may know, with greater accuracy, exactly what to guard against, if we are to forestall the concocting of similar medicine in America." [4] Certainly a principal aim of the study of public discourse is to enable us to participate fully in the communicative process, both as clear, effective persuaders, and as intelligent, hard-headed receivers of persuasion.

Public discourse, if studied carefully, may also demonstrate the ways in which man conciliates and compromises. Each day the world is slightly different from the world of the day before. New generations encounter old problems with new dimensions; change is incessant and inevitable. Rhetoric is directly concerned with the way men use symbols to encounter and influence change. Perceptions of

---

[4] Kenneth Burke, *The Philosophy of Literary Form: Studies in Symbolic Action*, rev. ed., New York: Random House, 1957, Vintage Books ed., p. 164.

reality and visions of the ideal vary greatly from person to person. When men attempt to influence their fellows and so direct the course of progress, goals and methods clash. The civilizing function of persuasive rhetoric is to mediate the aims of combatants and to motivate action that is consistent with the interest and survival of society. Broken heads and burned buildings are the result of a less civilized, more coercive rhetoric.

The success of persuasion is usually not total, nor is it immediate. The rhetorical process does not yield the ultimate solution, nor does it normally end in absolute victory for one side and rout for the other. Ideas and behavior may be long in changing and complete conversion is rare enough to be dramatic. Such a process has its vices and virtues.

Those who call for immediate and total reformation of behavior and elimination of evils experience deeply the frustration that comes from the failure to move men to act on professed ideals. Critics of persuasion as it operates in a democratic country frequently maintain that the process allows injustice and inhumanity to remain intact too long, that it is prone to sacrifice people to orderliness, that it is unable to foresee and thus forestall crisis let alone react quickly to solve serious and dangerous problems. There is obviously some degree of validity in such charges. But if progress in a democracy is to be steady and gains lasting, if all sides are to be heard and the rights of all protected, the initiation of reform must be accompanied by the preservation of what is good as well as the destruction of what is evil. The persuasive process is one of sifting and sorting ideas in a search for what is best. Persuasive rhetoric is not a weapon for bludgeoning the opposition with the club of revealed and absolute truth. Such a concept, however, should never be taken to mean that passionate advocacy is wrong, or that men cannot or should not argue forcefully for what they believe to be right. On the contrary, without the clash of strongly defended and articulated arguments, without the presentation of clearly defined alternatives, there would be no distinct ideas to sift and sort. Viewing persuasive discourse from a sound rhetorical perspective implies, rather, the exercise of mature and critical reflection—*action* is not suspended, *final, ultimate judgment,* however, is. After the delegates to the Constitutional Convention of 1789 had sweltered through the hot Philadelphia summer and drafted, finally, what was to become the Constitution of the United States, the time came for the document to be signed. The Convention debates had been vigorous and the final result was not completely to everyone's liking.

Benjamin Franklin, eighty-two years old, with years of experience as a politician, diplomat, and philosopher, defended the product of sixteen weeks' deliberation. He confessed that "there are several parts of this Constitution which I do not at present approve," but, he added, "I am not sure I shall never approve them. For, having lived long, I have experienced many instances of being obliged, by better information or fuller consideration, to change opinion, even on important subjects, which I once thought right, but found to be otherwise." [5] Viewing methods of changing, improving, and safeguarding our society from a rhetorical perspective is, essentially, understanding the possiblity of and need for "fuller consideration" of most questions that are really important. The man or woman who has developed a rhetorical perspective looks with skeptical eye on those who claim to be custodians of revealed truth and who hold that *their* fundamental beliefs may never be open to question. The student of rhetoric becomes atuned to the ways in which men accommodate each other as they live in a world of strain and change.

Values, aspirations, wildest dreams, in order to be meaningful must be communicated. Rhetoric makes functional what might otherwise be vague, unperceived, or misinterpreted. The feelings and hopes of a small band of colonists locked in a struggle against a great kingdom, were verbalized, and thus made the concrete, lasting aims of a nation, by Thomas Jefferson in the "Declaration of Independence" and Thomas Paine in "The Crisis." The throwing of a Molotov cocktail is undoubtedly a communicative act, but it is only when Stokely Carmichael's or Malcolm X's speeches put the act into the broad context of the struggle for racial justice that it can be understood, related to the history and image of American society, and evaluated. Failure to understand what men have stated publicly to their fellowmen leads to failure to understand the aspirations and perceptions of men since they began to organize and civilize their communal lives. The anthropologist puzzling over the ways in which ancient, simple man prepared what food he had, painstakingly examines the pots, the spoons, the utensils for sustaining life. Speeches are the artifacts of man's thought and vision. Their careful study will tell us something of where man has been and where he hopes to go.

When men began to live together in communities they began to substitute, in various ways and to varying extent, persuasion for

[5] Saul K. Padover, ed., *The Living United States Constitution,* New York: Mentor Books, 1953, p. 19.

brute force. A man's own fate, and perhaps the fate of hundreds of his fellow citizens, might turn on his ability to convince others. As this reality became increasingly apparent, curious men began to study rhetoric to determine the principles that operated to produce success. They have pondered over this problem for well over 2000 years and they are pondering still.[6]

Centuries of study and speculation have led scholars and practitioners of public communication to posit certain basic principles. Needless to say, any rhetorical principles are themselves constantly subjected to theoretical, philosophical, and empirical scrutiny—it would be absurd for rhetoricians to argue that they had found the ultimate answers to persuasion. Nevertheless, there are supportable generalizations that can be made and proposed as principles to guide the beginning student of rhetoric. These principles have two distinct functions: When studied carefully and applied they can improve the quality and effectiveness of an individual communicator, and, just as importantly, they provide tools the consumer of communication can use in evaluating persuasion. Struggling as he always is to control his environment, man is an influencing animal. We seek to influence others and we are influenced by others. This state of constant mutual influencing is neither good nor bad, it simply *is*. The principles of speaking, which are discussed in the following chapter, may be viewed as useful guides in this uniquely human enterprise of communicating and reacting to communication. They come from and may be understood more fully through the study of actual speeches. For by studying the principles as they operate in the speeches we can begin to isolate factors that are worthy of imitation and factors that direct our behavior.

[6] For a good brief survey of the development of speaking theory, see John F. Wilson and Carroll C. Arnold, *Public Speaking as a Liberal Art,* 2d ed., Boston: Allyn and Bacon, 1968, chap. 2. A thorough, in-depth study of the history of rhetorical theory and criticism is found in Lester Thonssen, A. Craig Baird, and Waldo W. Braden, *Speech Criticism,* 2d ed., New York: Ronald, 1970. See also the excellent chapter on "Rhetorical Theories of Persuasion" in Gary Cronkhite's *Persuasion: Speech and Behavioral Change,* Indianapolis: Bobbs-Merrill, 1969. An excellent short statement of the rhetorical perspective also appears in George A. Borden, Richard B. Gregg, and Theodore Grove, *Speech Behavior and Human Interaction,* Englewood Cliffs, N.J.: Prentice-Hall, 1969, pp. 179–197.

2
Practical
and Critical
Principles

If public communication is to take place, certain elements must be present. Any spokesman, whether he aims to secure a vote, sell a car, reinforce a religious belief, or create a feeling about war, plans what he will say with an audience in mind. Any set of principles must take into account the centrality of the relationships between a *speaker* and an *audience,* and a *message.* And, because the message is delivered under particular circumstances, communication must be understood in relation to its *context.*

The six principles discussed in this chapter focus on the investigation and description of these invarients (speaker, audience, message, context) in public discourse. The principles are: (1) a speech is designed for an audience; (2) a speech promotes identification between the audience and the topic; (3) a speech promotes identification between the audience and the speaker; (4) ideas and evidence in the speech must withstand the careful scrutiny of reasonable men; (5) the speech follows a pattern suitable to an audience, occasion, and topic; and (6) the speech employs a clear and appropriate style.

As was pointed out in the last chapter, these principles are not immutable rules. Rather, an understanding of these basic insights about the process of public communication will contribute to the development of the rhetorical perspective from which speeches can be both prepared and critically evaluated.

A speech is designed for an audience

One of the most basic of rhetorical facts is simply stated and yet has implications that are far-reaching: The purpose of a speech is to gain a desired response from an audience. Speech-making involves *getting* just as much as giving. That is, everything that a speaker does—what he says, what he does not say, how he moves, the tone of his voice—is likely to produce some kind of *response* from those who listen. His monotonous voice may put them to sleep, his lively sense of description might keep them interested, his vivid relation of a personal experience might frighten or amuse them. Everything that the speaker gives will get something in return. The skillful speaker plans what he *wants* to get and designs his speech to achieve his end, not just to give a performance.

The key, then, to designing a speech for an audience lies in understanding the crucial role of *purpose*. One of the most difficult tasks that faces a speaker is in trying to determine not only what he *wishes* to achieve, but also what he thinks is *possible* to accomplish. The particular group addressed and the context in which the speech takes place exert a real influence on the formation of a purpose. Take, for instance, an idea proposed a few years ago. During a discussion of ways in which U.S.–U.S.S.R. relations could be improved, a speaker suggested that Russia be invited to send lecturers to address service clubs such as Kiwanis, Lions, and Optimists. Such an act, he asserted, might demonstrate to the Russians our sincere belief in the right to public debate and might help us understand Soviet society. If the Soviets themselves ever felt confident enough to reciprocate, that would be an added bonus. The advocate of this plan asserted that we have very little to fear in providing a forum for Russian propaganda; he could not imagine a Kiwanis club being converted to communism by a luncheon talk, no matter how interesting or persuasive. And this, of course, is quite true. In some situations it is almost certain that drastic shifts in opinion will not be achieved. Does this mean, however, that nothing positive can be brought about in an encounter between a speaker and an audience with a distinctly different opinion? No, it only means that dramatic goals and the hopes for total conversion are usually in vain. A hypothetical visiting speaker from Moscow might convince an audience of American businessmen to travel in Russia, or to increase trade between the two countries, or even that it was not the goal of Soviet foreign policy to make good Marxists out of loyal Rotarians or to destroy the United States.

A speaker's perception of purpose is crucial for all that follows. The aim of the speech must affect the selection and handling of material. If it does not, the likely result is confusion and diffusion, to the discomfort of the audience and the distress of the speaker. Take, for example, a speaker whose aim it was to get listeners to agree with him that the Panama Canal Zone should be maintained as a U.S. territory. If this speaker were to spend a considerable amount of time describing the operation of the Canal locks (no matter how well he did this), he would have contributed little to the accomplishment of his purpose. It is also quite conceivable that the speaker could have held the audience rapt with a vivid retelling of the agonies and triumphs of the men who engineered and built the Canal. An audience could have been honestly delighted with such an "interesting" speech—but "interest" is not the end. Too many speakers are "interesting" but not memorable and not persuasive. A dull speaker is not likely to get very far, certainly, but even an interesting speaker must realize that material is subordinate to purpose.

Public discourse is considerably complicated by the fact that the audience is not always precisely definable. The audience that is physically present may not be the primary audience. The politician faces this acute problem almost daily; it is a fact of his political life. A politician once joked about himself by saying that whenever anyone asked him how he stood on the Civil Rights bill he answered unequivocally, "Where are you from?" The national politician's plight is that different people in different places often have different viewpoints and opinions, and the mass media can carry messages to several places at once. It might be hypothesized, for example, that Barry Goldwater's acceptance speech in 1964 was aimed at his immediate audience and not at the wider television audience. After a convention marked by the exchange of bitter hostilities between the "conservative" Goldwater Republicans and the "liberal" Rockefeller forces, the nominee's rejection of those who did not believe in the conservative cause and his seeming defense of extremism "in the cause of liberty" brought hundreds of cheering adherents to their feet. But the resounding words echoing throughout San Francisco's Cow Palace did not necessarily have the same effect throughout the country. A liberal eastern Republican might well have felt the burning sensation of salt being applied to his wounds. In short, what was good for the immediate audience of the faithful might not have been so for the general audience.

The fact that different audiences quite frequently do not have the same orientations, and respond differently to the same material and method of presentation, is a constant factor in designing messages for audiences. It would appear obvious that one can express the same idea in a variety of ways. Certainly a teacher, much of whose life is devoted to public discourse, learns that students at different levels have different experiences and different technical sophistication; one can discuss the same topic—cell growth, for example—with a high-school biology class, with freshmen in a required college course, with a graduate seminar, and although the topic might be the same there will have to be differences in the selection and presentation of materials. Anyone who has ever described the same experience or event to a good friend, a parent, a small brother or sister, knows very well that the nature of the audience has a significant impact on the speaker's choices.

If it is true that different audiences call for different approaches, how much then is the problem intensified when a speaker faces a wide and divergent audience? For one thing, the pressures toward blandness and ambiguity are intense. It is a great temptation—it might be argued, even a political necessity—to attempt to offend as few people as possible. Such an effort, of course, leads public discourse away from a real discussion of difficult issues. The use of slogans, image-building, and ambiguities become the currency of discourse when a speaker seeks to be all things to all men. The essential paradox in the impulse of a leader to speak to all men is that he may well end up by speaking to no one. Yet on the other extreme one finds would-be persuaders lessening their potential influence by ignoring completely the values, standards, and opinions of many who hear them. Sometimes this occurs through ignorance or narrowness of vision—fatal flaws in those who would shape the opinions of others. A small group of radical students at a large urban university, for example, seriously discussed the ways in which they should handle a campaign among construction workers on a nearby project. They allowed the doctrinaire position that students and workers were in natural alliance against the ruling classes to blind their perception of the rhetorical situation. They failed to take into account the realities of their potential audience. Their concentration on the issues as they perceived them (and how they posited that the audience *ought* to conceive them) led them to neglect the ways in which messages need to be geared to people and to assume that people gear themselves to messages. When construction workers in

New York attacked students at a peace rally in Wall Street, the radical organizers were disabused and severely disappointed, and their campaign was aborted. Had they pressed on with their plans, bloodshed could have occurred; what could not have occurred was persuasion.

Still, public discourse, even with the impelling need to take in many different auditors, does not have to be pallid, dreary stuff; nor does it need to be characterized by vicious, verbal blood-letting. Speaking to a wide audience may inspire an orator to heights of universality. The truly great speeches address intensely significant problems in a meaningful, lasting way.

Now certainly a speech designed for an audience is intended to influence that particular audience. But deep human problems and aspirations can be articulated with insight and vision. The kinds of situations that call forth public discussion and debate are rooted not only in the concerns of a time but also in the concerns of all time. A genuine attack on contemporary problems may often encompass universal qualities. Dr. King's moving description of his "dream" spoke to the problems of Civil Rights in America in 1963 and was designed as part of a massive effort to influence specific legislation. But that speech was much more than eloquent lobbying; it probed the depths of American conscience and interpreted the plight of the black man during centuries of the American experience. It was not just a speech to the thousands massed before the Lincoln Memorial or even to the millions who watched on their television screens. It was a speech to all men in all time who were concerned with the questions of justice and equality of opportunity. The great speaker is a man of his time, lives within his time, is a product of his time, and labors to solve the problems of his time; yet, the great speaker also has great vision, which transcends his time and penetrates the human condition. Turning Lincoln's observation around might better describe the potencies and realities of great rhetoric: When Gettysburg is recalled it may be that the specifics of what was done there become hazy if not forgotten, while what he said there the world will note and long remember.

The audience for a public speech may consist of those in the immediate presence of a speaker, those who will see him via television, those who will read his remarks, and those who will hear from others what he has said. For these groups, or that part of the potential audience best suited to respond and contribute to the accomplishment of the speaker's aims, the speaker addresses his

efforts. If the speaker is a great one, he may strike the universal
chord, and his words and thought may reach audiences unbounded
by time and place.

The concept that public discourse is designed to be heard and
reacted to by an audience does not imply that one audience may be
fully persuaded by one speech. This point will be developed more
fully below, but it needs to be emphasized that rarely is persuasion
the result of one speech. Changes, when they do come about, are not
usually the exclusive result of attending to twenty minutes or an
hour of discourse. One speech normally *contributes*, in varying
degrees, to the modification of attitudes and behavior; it does not
cause it. A speech designed for an audience takes into account not
only who the audience is (or audiences are), but what can reasonably
be expected of them.

The speaker   The speaker who wishes to put the principle that
a speech is designed for an audience into operation is faced with a
basic question, which he must attempt to answer: "Where does the
audience stand in relation to my topic?"

An auditor filters a speaker's message through a complicated series
of attitudes, opinions, perceptions, and experiences. To influence
listeners, the speaker must be aware of the influences already at
work on them. A successful speaker thinks very carefully about how
this configuration will affect the presentation of his ideas. The story
is told, for example, of a Government agency that attempted to
discover the effectiveness of propaganda that accused the United
States of germ warfare during the Korean War. An examination of
the results of a survey indicated that on one small island 99 percent
of the population did not believe the charge. One bureaucrat,
impressed by the overwhelming rejection of enemy propaganda,
investigated further. The cause of this resounding vote of confidence
was deflating to the unhappy official: No one on the island had ever
heard of germs! This story may be apocryphal, but the point is a
valid one for a speaker. Certain audiences cannot be persuaded on
certain matters because their total environment virtually makes it
impossible. If you do not have the slightest idea of what germs are,
there is little chance of convincing you that they are being used as a
weapon. However imperfectly he may be able to do so, the speaker
must try to reconstruct the framework within which the audience
operates. A common error that a beginning speaker makes is to
assume that members of the audience see the world as he does, or, if
they do not share his view of things, he may perceive his task as

simply "telling" them about it. Purposeful speaking, however, involves not "telling" an audience something but, rather, getting an audience to react. And reactions are influenced by the listener's total milieu.

Not only do audiences have their own perspectives, to which the speaker's material must be adapted, but members of the audience—like everyone else—play a wide variety of roles. An interesting psychological "game" might be called the "Who are you?" game. Ask someone the simple question, "Who are you?" and when he answers, ask him again, and again, until he just cannot think of anything more to say. You will get a long list of associations that the person thinks important, and not only will you begin to understand how he sees and identifies himself, what items are important to him, but also you will get an idea of the many roles we play and the many groups to which we belong. A speaker must realize that members of his audience hold several memberships and identifications. Sometimes a principal aim of a speaker will be to stress the importance of the values and ideas associated with one group to which many in the audience belong. He may hope to bring to the fore one set of values in order to neutralize another. The Women's Liberation Movement, for example, emphasizes and tries to separate out of the traditional culture the female's human role as distinct from the mother role, the wife role. Against some of the traditional values of society that stress and reinforce the woman's place in building a home environment, the liberationists would emphasize equally respectable and strong values of our society: those that put great store on individual freedom and the development of the full potential of the total human personality. Their rhetorical strategy is not necessarily to create new values but rather to view old ones from a new perspective. They would argue that the long-held and professed goals of American society—liberty and justice for all—have only been partially and imperfectly applied in the past and, if taken seriously, are in conflict with the established view of women primarily as homemakers and only secondarily as professionals. Their rhetorical aim must be to force their audience—both men and women—to perceive the contradictory nature of held values. They may hope to make men who, in their roles as husbands, wish a well-ordered and economically run home, recognize that such a position may generate values different from those associated with their role as American citizens who profess a firm belief in individuality and freedom. This same strategy can be seen operating in much of the rhetoric of modern reform movements. It is, also, the strategy long employed by the preacher who hopes to confront his audience with the sometimes conflicting values of the Sunday churchgoer and the Monday businessman. The point is that a speaker must make a serious and thoughtful attempt to understand the variety of roles represented in his audience and the values, goals, and behavior associated with these roles. In essence, the speaker may often try to bring to the level of audience awareness those conflicts we all attempt to balance and minimize in our daily lives. Then, by seeking to reinforce those values important to the accomplishment of his purpose, the speaker attempts to set up priorities to guide actions.

By taking all that he knows and can find out about his audience into account, the speaker is engaged in the task of adapting his message to the audience. His own goals must be realistic, and he must analyze carefully his own values and aspirations vis-à-vis the audience. With an understanding of those who will hear his message, the speaker seeks for common areas of agreement, common goals. This is not to say that the speaker flatters his audience; he does not pander to their wishes. Adaptation is not prostitution. Adaptation is the genuine attempt on the part of the speaker to make whatever goes into a speech rhetorically meaningful to a specific audience.

The critic   The primacy of the audience in rhetoric gives direction to the critic of public discourse. In trying to understand what is happening, it is essential for the critic first to identify the audience.

The critic must know the specific audience to whom the speech is addressed. What do they do? Why are they gathered together? What kinds of aims do they have? People who form audiences have a variety of characteristics that are pertinent to understanding them. Speech textbooks often list such items as age, sex, socioeconomic status, political beliefs, religious affiliation as factors to consider in audience analysis. Certainly the critic who wishes to reconstruct an audience for a speech that has been given, or understand fully a speech he is listening to, needs to factor out those elements that make a difference in the rhetorical situation. For example, a speech on the draft, to an audience in its late teens and early twenties obviously would need to take into account variables related to age. Before examining the nature of speaker–audience interactions, the critic must have a clear profile of the immediate audience.

Of course, as was pointed out earlier, the audience for a speech may be more wide-ranging than simply those seated in front of a

speaker in an auditorium. Through the mass media the speaker's
message may be carried to a multitudinous and varied audience. The
critic who would examine and evaluate public discourse cannot
neglect the unseen ears and eyes—the nebulous, difficult to delineate
audience, which, to varying degrees and in varying ways, receives,
attends, and acts.

As one begins to describe and understand an audience, he begins
to see relationships between that audience and the speaker. There is
in communication, after all, a strong sense of mutuality. The speaker
hopes to direct and influence an audience; the audience, in its turn,
exerts a strong influence on the speaker's goals and choices. From a
careful study of relationships something of the speaker's perceptions
and values begins to emerge. Much can be learned about the speaker
himself by looking at the way he deals with an audience. The critic
may discern the answers to such questions as: Where does the
speaker perceive the locus of power to be? Who are the speaker's
identifiable kindred spirits—his heroes and his adherents? Who are
the speaker's clear enemies—his devils and his detractors?

Further, the critic can learn more of the speaker through the ways
in which he hopes to move his audience. The critic seeks to discover
the extent to which the speaker's appeals indicate a clear understanding of the audience and the members' backgrounds, goals,
emotions, and so forth. How the speaker uses his knowledge of the
audience should, the critic would reasonably assume, be patently
consistent with the speaker's purpose. The critic would be interested
in the ways that the speaker exploited or failed to exploit the nature
of the audience. A careful examination of the interaction might,
indeed, sharpen the critic's understanding of the speaker's true
purpose—a purpose that might not always be apparent to the casual
listener or even to the speaker himself.

Now what does this investigation begin to tell the critic, what
insights does it tend to develop? On the basis of the speaker's
interaction with the audience, the critic will begin to form a
judgment of the speaker's skill in dealing with available resources
and his perception of the rhetorical situation. Also, the analysis
begins to offer clues as to the speaker's ethical position. For as the
critic discovers those audience values that the speaker hopes to
reinforce and those he denigrates, as the critic identifies the forces
and personalities that the speaker praises or attacks, then the critic
begins to see clearly the speaker's views on proper and improper
modes of conduct and action.

At this point, of course, the critic's judgment is somewhat tentative; it may be refined or amended as other principles are investigated.

Much space has been here devoted to the principle that a speech is designed for an audience. That is because the understanding of the audience as central to public discourse is essential to the development of a rhetorical perspective. All the principles that follow are in some way related, either as refinements, elaborations, or extensions, of this cardinal one.

A speech promotes identification between the audience and the topic

For an audience to be moved by a message the topic under discussion must be meaningful to that audience. People can hardly be expected to modify their behavior or action if they do not see the relationship between them and the topic. It is only when involvement in the topic occurs that persuasion can take place. This means that the speech must make explicit the ways in which the audience can identify what is being advocated with its own experience.

There sometimes exists among intelligent people a strong suspicion of emotion. How often have we heard the admonition, "Don't be swayed by emotion," or even commented ourselves that a speaker was "emotional" and, hence, his conclusions not entirely to be trusted. But what is emotion, after all, but *involvement*? Can you imagine a topic about which you feel no emotion whatsoever? If so, is it possible for you to think of being convinced one way or another to take action relevant to that topic? Can you remember, for example, a boring conversation that you were a part of? What made it boring? It was probably boring because you were not really participating in the conversation. Perhaps people whom you did not know were being discussed. Maybe you are not a sports fan and the relative merits of two teams were being argued. Suppose, for example, you and a date found yourselves in a group of young married couples talking about conflicting methods of child rearing. If a child was present and was busily engaged in stirring your beer with his lollipop without being deterred by his mother, you might develop feeling on the topic under investigation because it involved you. Without a sense of identification, you would be bored and unlikely to take a position on the matter.

When an audience feels indignation, or sympathy, or anger, or love, then an audience is capable of being persuaded. When an audience is indifferent or apathetic little can be hoped for. Lack of student participation in university governance, for example, is often the despair of student leaders. Reformers would argue that this is quite understandable, that student apathy is the result of a realization that it does not make any difference whatsoever who wins an election, that it is a game to amuse the few and to make students think that they share in the decision-making process. Whether or not student government is, indeed, frequently the fraud that its critics claim it to be, many students feel no emotional commitment to its continuance and support. When that is the case, it is very hard to get out the vote.

Emotional involvement, then, is an absolutely necessary ingredient in successful public discourse. Emotion is human, and in and of itself neither bad nor good. Take the emotion of fear, for example. Is it morally reprehensible for a speaker to attempt to arouse in his audience fear of the effects of the use of heroin? Should we not fear the results that may derive from the total disregard of the ecological balance of nature? Of course, fears of the unknown and fears for our own personal safety may be exploited to promote division and hatred between men. Consider, as a further illustration, the judicial process. Judgments are to be made on the facts alone, on the evidence presented in court. Even given this principle to be a sound one, could it be argued that understanding, sympathy, mercy should *never* play a part in the final judgment? Or could it be argued that feelings of revenge, hostility, or prejudice *never* infect the process of decision? The *way* in which emotions are appealed to or manipulated is a legitimate moral concern; but those who would participate in any way in public discourse must realize that emotions are not, per se, evil—without them there is no persuasion.

The emotional process of identification is facilitated when the audience can relate directly to the values and ideals expressed through the speech. For example, it is possible to talk about birth control or abortion within the context of population control. While many members of a given audience might find these methods in conflict with held values, other values might be posed in opposition. It is possible to conceive of varying degrees of argument or justification being admitted by even an initially unsympathetic audience. But to propose infanticide as a remedy for overpopulation would be so alien to the values of our culture, so far beyond the limits of the total configuration of values of the audience, that it is doubtful that the speaker would have any chance at all of being heard. Certainly, the value appeals and the symbols used that aid identification are those in which the audience puts faith and trust.

The speaker   The speaker's role in promoting identification between the audience and the topic stems from his understanding of the audience and his capacity to design the speech with them in mind. When the speaker has discerned the needs and goals of the audience and understands how audience motivations are related to such factors as group memberships and roles, then he can establish the lines of involvement. Often the speaker will need to probe deeply to uncover motivations. We have all heard of the "hidden agenda," the unstated reasons we might not even be totally aware of ourselves yet that determine our actions. The good speaker devotes considerable energy and thought to the source of stated beliefs and feelings. An audience that may be expected to identify with topics related to quality education, for example, may be markedly apathetic or uninterested in a serious discussion. A thoughtful speaker may rightly speculate that the topic seems irrelevant because the audience assumes that there is nothing wrong with current practice, or because they feel their well-being more threatened by a possible increase in property taxes than by the deteriorating quality of schools. Their roles as taxpayers may, given the right set of circumstances, overshadow their role as parents. The speaker investigates his audience's network of associations and loyalties to determine which springs must be tapped if the listeners are to identify with the topic at hand.

With the aim of further audience identification with the topic in mind, the speaker will make his choices carefully. Whenever possible, material chosen supports this aim: Language, appeals, evidence—all contribute to identification. Examples, for instance, would be selected with an eye to the audience's principal concerns; appeals to loyalty might be made to those who associate themselves with patriotic organizations; the appropriate use of such terms as "individuality" and "relevance" might serve to alert certain audiences to the fact that values they hold strongly are under discussion.

The critic   The critic strives to uncover the values expressed—implicitly or explicitly—and to understand the appeals to identification that are at work in public discourse. In his search for the emotional base from which the audience is responding, the critic examines the emotional appeals upon which the audience-topic identification is based. Why certain topics are interesting or appealing, why audiences attend to specific topics, and how the speaker stresses those elements that invite attention are fundamental to understanding what is happening in the communication process. A topic is not necessarily inherently interesting; that is the point made throughout this section. The skilled persuader finds the proper chord to pluck and the critic asks why this is proper and how the speaker came to choose it given the options open to him.

As he investigates the possible causes of audience identification, the critic uncovers relationships between values embedded in the topic, the values of the audience, and the values of contemporary society. If, for example, a strong cultural value is professed for individuality and a critic finds extensive evidence of appeals to conformity used successfully to promote identification, he may begin to observe and substantiate the breakdown or modification of societal values. An examination of the rhetorical realities of audience identification will disclose significant information about the workings of a society and its practical moral code.

A speech promotes identification
between the audience and the speaker

Communication is facilitated when an audience has trust, respect, and confidence in a speaker. Throughout the history of the development of rhetorical theory, students of persuasion have recognized the potency of personal appeal. The classical term used to describe the force of the speaker's personality on the imagination and action of the audience is "ethos," and this term is still most frequently employed in contemporary writings on speech. The early Greek and Roman theorists thought of ethos as essentially related to the character of the speaker; the proposals and policies of a good man would be more likely to carry weight with an audience than would those of one who was disreputable. But as theory developed, scholars began to realize that the "true" nature of a man may or may not be *perceived* by an audience. A speaker's ethical position is filtered through the screen of the audience's perception of the speaker's character and motives. Ethos, then, is *not* synonymous with ethics. The way the audience views the character of the speaker, the audience's assessment of the speaker's intelligence, the audience's judgment of the speaker's sincerity—these are the ingredients of the speaker's ethos. Some Americans, for example, think of Richard Nixon as a wise and courageous political leader who has achieved the Presidency despite great obstacles; others cannot and will never think of him as anyone but "Tricky Dick." Undoubtedly Mr. Nixon's character is complex and many-sided. There are unquestionably facets of his personality that tend to support the conclusions of both his admirers and critics. But, even though it is not easily discerned or described, Mr. Nixon has something that might be called his "true" character. Yet this "true" character is not what is of the most serious rhetorical interest. The character of a man may be considered fixed at a given moment, but at the same moment his ethos may vary radically according to the audience responding to his rhetorical overtures. Mr. Nixon's ethos can be positive or negative, depending on who is making the determination. As is quite obvious, an unfavorable ethos will hamper the effectiveness of a speaker, whereas a favorable ethos may well be the single most potent force in promoting successful persuasion.

Much has been said and written in recent years about the political art of "image" making. In effect, marketing and advertising techniques, long in use in commercial fields, have been imported into the political arena. The aim of the image-builder is to create a favorable ethos for his candidate. Now this is not an entirely new factor in public communication. Machiavelli's advice to *The Prince* contains numerous suggestions on actions that a ruler might take in order to create a public image that will help him hold his subjects in check. History is studded with examples of men who have used their powerful personalities to assume and hold power. The growing pervasiveness of the mass media, coupled with the increased sophistication of psychological and motivational techniques, has raised some serious ethical concerns about the manipulation of ethos.

It must be realized, however, that ethos is a quality that exists on all levels of communication. We have all taken actions at one time or another because someone whom we trust and whose judgment we respect has advised us to do so, even if no other evidence is available. Conversely, we sometimes find ourselves observing that, if *"he* is in favor of it, I'm against it." If a speaker suggests a solution to a troublesome problem and we know that speaker to be a thoughtful and reputable expert in the area under discussion, can it seriously be argued that our awareness of his experience and knowledge should not be allowed to influence in any way our decision? We know that in the realm of interpersonal relations we cannot help but rely to some extent on ethos. In our daily lives we face different audiences as we play different roles. What others see of us and hear of us and learn about us affects the ethos we have for them. And certainly we create and make use of this ethos as we communicate.

Because of his background or his past relations with the audience a speaker may bring with him an image that affects the audience's reactions. Furthermore, what occurs in the speech and in the speaking situation may also significantly affect the speaker's ethos. A student in a beginning public speaking class, for example, rose and went quietly to the front of the room when his turn to speak came. He carried with him a brown paper bag. Without saying a word, he took from the bag a hammer and wrapped it in a cloth, which he likewise produced from the bag. He walked purposefully to the window, and, with a swift stroke, he broke a small pane of glass. The audience was shocked and unnerved. The speaker went on to explain how to replace a window pane, removing the necessary materials for repair from the bag as he spoke. He had planned carefully, measuring the window beforehand. His intention had been to capture the attention of the audience by a dramatic initial gesture. It is doubtful, however, that anyone in the audience learned what he wished them to learn by listening to his speech. The action had been too unexpected, too bizarre, and the audience was somewhat trau-matized. The effect on his future speeches was unfortunate. He was thought of as the class eccentric, not to be taken too seriously, and there was discernible nervousness among the audience each time he got up to speak. By an action the audience thought to be extreme, he had impaired his ethos. But another speaker, by clear and interesting accounts of technical matters, established himself as an authority in the class on scientific questions; his speeches created for him an ethos that often caused other members of the class to turn to him to resolve disputes or give his opinion on technical questions.

So the speaker may create or bring with him a negative or positive ethos. Some speakers may have a stronger ethos for some audiences, but ethos itself cannot be ignored as an instrumental force in persuasion.

The speaker   As in all aspects of his relations with his audience, the speaker must anticipate. He must attempt to see himself through the eyes of the audience. He must ask himself what the audience might know or think about his own background, his views, his position on the topic under consideration. If his own experience qualifies him in a special way to discuss the topic he should, perhaps through the use of a personal example, let the audience know of his unique relation to the topic. If he plans to take a position in conflict with the one that he reasonably assumes the audience to hold, it might be necessary first to reinforce attitudes or beliefs the speaker and audience hold in common, to examine first areas of agreement before proceeding to advocate controversial ideas.

Recognition of sources of hostility or of support gives a speaker clues as to appropriate strategy. Disagreement cannot be avoided; but disagreement that occurs in an atmosphere of hostility and rancor is unlikely to be resolved. A noted educator once addressed a small audience of academics on the topic of unilateral initiatives for peace. When the talk was finished, the chairman asked for questions. In the audience was a prominent philosopher who had taken positions publicly that were in obvious disagreement to those just espoused by the speaker. When the philosopher rose to ask a question, the speaker commented, "Ah, Professor Smith, I know how concerned you are with this question, and I am honored that you have come to listen to me. I am most interested in your reactions." The professor paused, then smiled and observed candidly, "I'm disarmed." He then went on to raise several penetrating questions, but the spirit was clearly one of inquiry and honest doubt, not of attack. He even listened patiently and thoughtfully to the answers.

It is important for the speaker to realize that ethos does not suddenly appear out of nowhere; it does not exist in a vacuum. All that a speaker does and is contributes to his ethos. Audiences, for example, get visual impressions that affect their perceptions. A speaker can *look* confident or uncomfortable, neat or sloppy, serious or flippant. A whole series of nonverbal clues can suggest a speaker's attitude toward the audience. These impressions, together with what the speaker says and the way he says it go to forming the speaker's ethos in a given situation. Most of us do not appear before audiences with a national reputation and a known position on a wide spectrum of issues. But we do bring with us our own relevant knowledge, interests, attitudes, and associations from which ethos is created.

The critic   In order to understand the total persuasive milieu, the critic must identify the role played by the speaker's ethos. He seeks to discover what assets and liabilities the speaker brings with him or creates in a communication situation.

Knowledge of what the speaker has working for or against him will help the critic to appreciate the limitations imposed on the speaker. Speaking to a hostile audience, an advocate may, realistically, have little chance of bringing about a significant change of opinion. If the critic understands this, this insight may help the critic to fathom the speaker's purpose more clearly. It may help to explain why a speaker seemingly limited or refocused his goals in a way other than that which might be expected of him. Further, understanding a speaker's ethos might help to explain the speaker's success or failure. The old fable of the boy who cried wolf, for example, is a perfect study in the lack of persuasiveness resulting from a negative ethos. Even though the dreaded event really was occurring, even though the wolf was indeed in the fold, the boy's reputation for unfounded alarms destroyed his persuasiveness. Any attempt to understand completely the behavior of those who failed to heed the boy's cries that does not take into account the boy's established ethos are bound to be fruitless.

The extent to which the speaker relies on his image as a persuasive device is also of interest to the critic. Is identification, for example, used to supplement or to substitute for other evidence? At some time or another everyone is faced with the question: Should I believe it just because he says it is so? The critic hopes to discover in what ways and to what extent this question is answered affirmatively or negatively. It is possible, for example, to read the speeches of leaders such as Dwight Eisenhower or Douglas MacArthur and detect a strong tendency on the part of the speaker to rely on his personal experience and acknowledged success in military affairs. Indeed, an audience will often feel justified, even compelled, to react on the basis of the speaker's personal proof because much evidence is simply not available (e.g., classified material) or too diffuse and extensive to be attended to and comprehended.

The critic will also attempt to assess the speaker's image in the light of his expressed values, ideas, and appeals. In essence, this means that the critic will try to uncover the possible sources of personal influence. The values and ideas that the audience and the speaker share, and which the speaker exploits, and the nature of those appeals that seem to influence audiences and increase their positive feelings for the speaker, give direction to the critic who would unravel the threads of ethos in the persuasive weave.

Because nonverbal factors contribute in some way to the establishment of ethos, the critic examines them with some care. Much of what is known about the effects of nonverbal behavior in the rhetorical process is speculation, albeit some speculation is more sophisticated than other. The critic must, at least, develop an

awareness of the potential influences of the visual aspects of
message. Several years ago, for example, when Senator Joseph
McCarthy attacked the army for its alleged "softness" toward
Communism, a Senate Committee investigated the charges and
countercharges in what is now known as the Army–McCarthy
hearings. These hearings were nationally televised and avidly
watched throughout the country. While the hearings were going on
the story was told of a man who came home one afternoon to find
his two small children absorbed in the television proceedings. He
noticed in their excited account of events that they referred to the
"good guy" and the "bad guy." When asked to identify these
characters on the screen they readily pointed to McCarthy as "bad"
and Secretary of the Army Stephens as "good." It became clear in
the conversation that the children had not developed any political
partisanship; they could tell by *looking* who was good and who was
bad. The white to gray-haired Stephens in his immaculate, light-
colored suit was pitted against McCarthy in his dark, slightly
crumpled suit, appearing somewhat sinister with his five-o'clock
shadow. In many ways the antagonists resembled the white-hatted
Hopalong Cassidy and his black-hatted evil enemies in the William
Boyd films popular on television in the fifties. Just as the use of a
word may trigger many associated emotions and memories, so a
visual image has the potential for evoking a variety of reactions
which affect the speaker's image. Politicians certainly are aware of
the impact that their visual presentation via television has on the
electorate and have called on advertising agencies, and actors, to help
them individually and even in workshop settings. It has been
generally observed, for instance, that Richard Nixon's makeup in his
first televised debate in 1960 with John Kennedy may have
contributed to the poor image he projected.

The critic certainly cannot measure the effects of such visual
elements with anything approaching accurate certainty; he can,
however, sift carefully through what evidence is available and isolate
those factors that can reasonably be assumed to have played a part
in the formation of a speaker's ethos.

Ideas and evidence in the speech must withstand the careful scrutiny of reasonable men

Reason is a highly valued but somewhat ambiguous quality. The
term has taken on strong value qualities. Who wishes to be thought
of as unreasonable? Rational argument is good, irrationality is bad.

But reason itself is not easily defined, nor is it always clear when one is being reasonable.

At the root of the difficulty in dealing with reason is the commonly held notion that reason is absolute. Reason is sometimes equated with formal logic and is believed, accordingly, to follow a rigid set of immutable rules. But such is not the case in rhetorical logic. Reason in rhetoric is influenced and determined by at least two critical and relative factors: the assumptions of the audience and the foundation of argument in probability.

First, consider the assumptions of the audience. Because an audience is necessarily limited and bound by the time and place in which it exists, the historical and cultural context of a speech may influence considerations of reasonableness. In the contemporary Anglo-American culture, for example, a widely held, even revered, assumption is that representative democracy is a good—perhaps it would be accurate to say the best—form of government devised by man. A speaker holding this assumption, and deriving arguments from it, would not be thought to be unreasonable. One could build a "logical" argument against policies and leaders that sought to demonstrate that democratic principles were being subverted. A counterargument might be launched in an attempt to prove that the speaker's evidence did not substantiate the claim that democracy was in danger, that his conclusions did not flow logically from his arguments. But it would be highly unlikely that a counterargument would hold that the basic assumption was illogical; the strong positive cultural value of democracy is so great that few would even think to challenge it, nor would most audiences be prepared to entertain such a challenge. Yet in 1789 no such assumption was universally held. Much of the debate at the Constitutional Convention centered on ways to hold democracy in check, and few would have described themselves proudly as democrats. And in 1832 in England, when legislation aimed at enlarging the franchise was being debated, even the most ardent Whig proponents of reform were at pains to assure their audiences that they were not democrats—even that the passing of the Reform Bill would *prevent* democracy and its feared excesses. To have begun with the assumption that democracy is a positive good and to have argued from that premise would have been considered most "illogical" by the mass of auditors.

Now much of what is called agitation or even radical rhetoric attacks basic assumptions. It shocks and upsets many audiences. No matter what political outlook one may hold, if he has read or heard the words of such radical spokesmen as Abbie Hoffman or Eldridge Cleaver or Mark Rudd, he would not be likely to characterize their rhetoric as "logical." It seems that the basis for a negative judgment could well be intimately related to the radical propensity for attacking established values and assumptions or for arguing from assumptions that are rejected or misunderstood.

The basic point is simply this: Knowlege, perspective, and attitude shape assumptions and outlook; all these factors may cause audiences to define and perceive "reason" in different ways.

Furthermore, rhetorical logic is firmly based in the concept of probability. We rarely argue about certainties. We might disagree about the date of Woodrow Wilson's death; but we can settle that disagreement with an encyclopedia. What we might, indeed, wish to attempt to persuade each other about could be the lasting value of the League of Nations experiment that Wilson supported so strongly. Such an issue raises questions dealing with the *probable* reasons for and consequences of certain international actions. In most aspects of human conduct it is practically impossible to assign definite cause-effect relationships. When we examine the motivations of those around us—or our own motivations—we can rarely know with certainty why particular behaviors occur, but we can often hazard a good guess; based on the evidence we have at hand, for instance, we might be fairly certain that Jack left the room at the time he did to avoid seeing Ann. We think, on the basis of what we know of their relationship, that such an action is *probable*.

Much of what occurs in public communication is essentially prediction. We can urge that American policy in Asia follow a particular course because if it does not, such and such will be the *result*. Being logical in such circumstances is maintaining a strict internal consistency in a speech—that is, maintaining a clear predictive relationship between evidence and conclusions.

One will often hear of fallacious reasoning. Basically, this faulty logic occurs when the speaker's use of material in the speech is misleading and distorts the case. For example: John Smith has just proposed we each give $5.00 to the Red Cross. Harry Jones, in a speech following the Smith proposal, attacks John Smith as a man who is lazy and who is never willing to do his share of the work. Jones argues that Smith is not to be trusted and his proposition should be voted down. Now this obvious example often occurs more subtly, but it is a very common form of fallacious reasoning. It is what is referred to as an "ad hominum" argument (an argument against the man). Whatever Smith may be like, no matter how successful Jones is in establishing the fact that Smith is lazy, such evidence does not warrant the conclusion that we should not give $5.00 to the Red Cross. How often are proposals dismissed as unworthy even of serious consideration because the man who originated the idea is someone who is under attack *personally*? To take another, different kind of example: A speaker unfolds, in great detail, the story of an experience he had when driving across the country. He picked up a young man on the road who was hitchhiking. When they stopped at a diner for coffee, the young man slipped away, stole the older man's car, and was long gone before the theft was noticed. Now the kind of conclusion that the speaker reaches may be reasonable or unreasonable. He might conclude that it is dangerous to pick up hitchhikers. This is reasonable enough—such a conclusion does not claim that one will always have a bad experience, but only that the possibility exists, and the possibility is established by the personal experience. If the speaker wishes to reinforce the logic of his conclusion he will give testimony of the experience of others, perhaps cite statistics compiled by law enforcement agencies, and so forth. In other words, he will marshal the resources available to him to make his conclusion stand. If, however, the speaker, on the basis of the evidence of the example, concluded that young people today are thieves and are not to be trusted, he would have far exceeded the logical limits that his evidence warranted. The weight of such a sweeping generalization would crush such puny evidence. In short, in order for a speaker to be logical his evidence must establish that what is claimed is probable; if such is not the case, the reasoning is faulty.

The speaker   The speaker's task is to assemble the components of a speech in a logical manner. As in all aspects of public discourse, the speaker's principal attention is focused on the audience. He must explore the assumptions held by his listeners in order to understand what is considered reasonable by them. If the speaker holds assumptions quite alien to the audience, he should know this and not base arguments exclusively on premises that the audience cannot understand or accept.

How the speaker gathers and uses evidence is a measure of his ability to argue reasonably. The speaker may use examples, personal experiences, testimony of authority, statistics, analogy; he may present his material in a variety of visual and auditory ways, but no matter what is included or how it is presented, the touchstone of rhetorical logic is probability. The speaker chooses material that tends to show that what he proposes is the natural outcome of the observable facts and available information.

The critic   The critic attempts to ascertain the logical relationships in the speech. He first searches carefully for the speaker's and for the audience's assumptions. Only by uncovering these can the critic understand the common ground held by the speaker and those whom he hopes to persuade, and the basic divergences, which cause serious problems in successful communication. Such an investigation will provide clues for the critic as to how the speaker and audience view their world. Conclusions, for example, that are presented without any evidence whatsoever generally point to underlying convictions that the speaker considers so basic, that are so automatic, that they need no support at all. If such conclusions are readily accepted by an audience, then the audience apparently shares at least that aspect of the speaker's world-view.

When the critic probes the reason inherent in a speech he looks most closely at the nature of the evidence and its relationship to generalizations. First, each piece of evidence calls for the critic's careful scrutiny. Accuracy and recency are relevant criteria. Are statistics correct, for example, or does the testimony of a respected political leader represent his latest thinking on the problem, or are two plans being compared really comparable in the essential elements? If the evidence itself is in any way distorted, then the chances of reaching a confidently predictable conclusion are diminished.

If the evidence itself is acceptable, the critic then examines the projections of that evidence in the form of generalizations. Given the accuracy of supporting material, does that material allow one to move consistently to the conclusion? In the example cited above, Jones might have been quite accurate as to Smith's character weaknesses. He might have given several accurate and recent examples, he might have correctly quoted a number of leading citizens on the subject of Smith's lack of initiative. But this evidence was not pertinent: It did not address itself to the question at hand, it did not support the final generalization. So the critic's evaluation, then, involves investigating specific material and the relationships among the parts that make up the total argument. The nature of these relationships determines in large measure the reasonableness of the speech.

The speech adheres to a pattern suitable
to an audience, occasion, and topic

Public discourse may be impromptu, a spontaneous reaction to an
immediate rhetorical situation, it may be extemporaneous, prepared
and thought out but not planned in all specific details, or it may be a
manuscript speech in which the very language to be used has been
weighed and selected. No matter how formal or informal a speech,
some degree of structure is imposed if the speaker seeks to prevent
his message from sounding like hopeless ramblings.

A speech is not a random relation of information; order is created
within the limitations imposed. Time, space, and the physical setting
create limitations that might influence organization. If one has, for
example, five minutes to address an audience, the pattern of the
speech would be quite different from a speech made by one allotted
twenty minutes. When the speech is shorter, it might be necessary
for a speaker to move quickly and directly to his point rather than
approach the topic inductively. It may be, for instance, that a large
outdoor meeting will call for a simpler organizational pattern
because there is no opportunity to use charts or blackboards or
projectors or any other device to present the pattern for an audience
visually and to help them follow.

Further, the nature of the audience and the situation may suggest
relationships that call for certain organizational patterns. If a speaker
was addressing a group with a strong historical identity, an
established tradition by which it set great store, a group, perhaps,
that viewed continuity as a positive virtue, then the speaker might be
well advised to organize his material chronologically, showing the
growth and development of his plan over time, and thus demonstrating its consistency with the thinking and aims of the past.

Earlier in this chapter the essential role of purpose was discussed.
Purpose, which defines the relationship between the speaker and the
audience, also controls organization. Each idea that is to be
developed is tested by the comparison of its intent with the purpose
of the speech. An idea that does not further the purpose does not
belong in the speech. Ideas are, in turn, supported by material that
must pass a similar test: Evidence that does not make the idea more
believable does not belong in a supporting position. Thus the basic
pattern of a speech is determined by the intertwining relationships
between purpose, ideas, and supporting material.

The speaker   A speaker must understand the limitations and
work within them. Out of the potential chaos of ideas and evidence,

the speaker imposes order. A painter, faced with the restrictions of
canvas size, dimensionality, pigment combinations, and so forth,
creates a harmony and balance in spite of the restrictions. The
process of selection and arrangement is a highly imaginative and
artistic endeavor; events, for example, that took years to occur, must
be described and situated within the context of a ten-minute speech
in such a way that they become meaningful.

The speaker's chances of success are slim indeed if his crucial
ideas are lost in a mass of verbiage, if the relationships between ideas
become blurred, if the evidence upon which conclusions are based is
so detached or obscured that the juxtaposition of generalization and
support is lost, if the design is so intricate and ornate that a listening
audience cannot follow without excessive effort. Imposing an order
implies an effort on the part of the speaker to insure as far as
possible that he will provide the audience with a clear and direct
map to follow.

The method of planning a tight and careful organizational pattern
is usually some form of outlining. If outlining is thought of as a kind
of skeleton of the speech, a manner of summary, then outlining will
probably not be helpful. Outlining is, however, *a way of going about*
the patterning of material. If the speaker keeps in mind the
relationship of purpose to main ideas to evidence (discussed above),
he will actually build an outline as he goes along. For example, if a
speaker's purpose is to gain the agreement of his audience to the
proposition that heart disease may be prevented, he might well
submit that heart disease can be prevented by getting proper
exercise, by eating the correct diet, and by giving up or not starting
smoking. The speaker will find that medical opinion strongly
supports the need for exercise. He may read an article in a leading
magazine that quotes a famous heart specialist as saying that proper
exercise is the best way of preventing heart attack. He may find a
similar statement from the American Medical Association. He may
read the case history of a cardiac patient whose problem was
diagnosed as directly related to a lack of exercise. And so he would
proceed through masses of material sorting and choosing that which
is most pertinent to the purpose. As he does so, an outline is actually
developing, and adding numbers to material serves merely to keep
everything in its proper relationship. Just with the material
mentioned thus far, the speaker would have the beginning of an
outline as follows:

> I. Heart disease can be prevented by proper exercise.
>   A. Medical opinion holds that exercise is vital.
>   1. A heart specialist maintains that . . .
>   2. The AMA has issued a statement that holds that . . .
>   B. Mr. X was a cardiac patient whose problem was diagnosed . . .
> II. Eating the correct foods will help prevent heart attacks.
> III. Smoking is likely to increase the chances of contracting heart disease.

Much, of course, remains to be done. But the outline is the surest and most thorough method to help the speaker understand the way in which his material fits into patterns, and it shows him what unnecessary material may be pruned and what essential material seems to be missing.

Further, the speaker who is aware of his audience considers what effect its members might have on his organizational planning. If, for instance, a speaker expects that an audience will be hostile to his basic idea, he may wish to plan an indirect method of development in which he stresses common assumptions, goals, and beliefs and moves inductively to the point at issue. This manner of organization may at least insure that the audience will listen to the speaker and perhaps develop a respect for his ideas, or the quality of his thinking, or his skill in relating to them, before the potentially divisive idea is broached. This is preferable to an immediate declaration that arouses the hostility of an audience and is likely to cause auditors to stop listening, perhaps to expend their efforts at rebuttal by carrying on a running internal debate with the speaker. And the results of such a debate would hardly be expected to be favorable to the speaker.

The critic   The critic investigates the relationships between the pattern of arrangement and the speaker's and audience's ideas and assumptions. He first locates and identifies important ideas. An examination of these ideas will give additional evidence about the speaker's motives and goals. Patterning might further suggest the primacy of ideas within a given setting.

The critic then proceeds to assess the degree to which the speaker has adjusted his organization to the needs of the setting and the audience. Within the imposed limits the speaker has been compelled to manage ideas; the critic attempts to understand the

ways in which the speaker has done this and to judge the intellectual
skill with which he has balanced purpose, ideas, and evidence.

The speech employs a clear and appropriate style

Style is one of the most difficult of communication concepts with
which to deal. It is difficult theoretically because a clear and
generally accepted view of style does not exist. Scholars in
the fields of speech, English, and linguistics are actively and ardently
searching for a definitive description of style and its distinction from
content, but the issue is complex and complicated. There are,
however, some basic ideas about style that are important and useful
to the speaker and to the critic.

Certainly the most crucial element of style in public discourse is
the use of language. Some still assume that language "clothes"
ideas—that language is a kind of decoration added to
thought, or a way of channeling thought from oneself to others.
However, it seems more fruitful to realize the nature of language as
both reflective of and influencing thought. The words we choose
indicate the way we perceive and feel about much that is around us.
In political discourse, for example, the use of adjectives may give
significant clues as to how the speaker sees himself and his opponents. One speaker may assert that "the liberal forces in this country
are firmly behind this plan," whereas another speaker maintains that
"this proposal is supported by the left-wing elements in this
country." The use of "liberal" or "left-wing" signals a very different
view of the proponents of the plan. "Liberal" suggests that the user
sees those who support the plan as forward looking, progressive, a
part of the American political tradition of innovation and improvement, whereas the user of "left wing" sees the proposal's backers as
radical, out of the main stream, even subversive of traditional
American values. One who has identified a speaker or a movement as
"left wing" will react in a different way to persuasion emanating
from that group than will one who has identified them as "liberal."

The *way* in which things are said is intimately related to who and
what the speaker is. It has been suggested, for example, that
Vice-President Agnew played the primary partisan political role
in the Nixon Administration, that in his speaking tours, he addressed
the party faithful to reinforce their beliefs and allegiance to
conservative principles. His word choice reflected clearly this role.
The Vice-President's unique style was obviously not designed to
convert the opposition, but to draw positive responses from those

who saw the enemy attacked without verbal quarter. To take
another example: During the Columbia disturbances of 1968, Mark
Rudd, the SDS chairman, rose to a position of leadership among
radical students. As he stood before a large crowd of supporters and
sympathizers, in the heat of excitement and revolutionary fervor, he
considered with his audience the proposals sent from the vice-president of the university. One cannot imagine Mr. Rudd saying that
"the proposals sent by Mr. Truman are an inadequate basis for
discussion, and we reject them." What he did say was much more
reflective of his thought and the thought of his supporters; his reply
expressed the contempt in which they held the university administration and the overwhelming feelings of rejection they directed
toward proposals for negotiation. His choice of words said much
about his own position; he merely replied, "Bullshit," and the crowd
roared its approval.

In short, language is not only means but it is also substance. A
speaker's style is essentially a culmination of other rhetorical
factors, for it indicates much about the speaker's view of the
audience and situation, about how the audience identifies with the
topic, about how the audience identifies with the speaker.

Style itself has a persuasive force of its own, although all the
factors that make up style are not clear. The "Kennedy style,"
for example, was obviously more than the President's use of
language alone. His particular way of pronouncing words, his
handsome appearance, his quick, confident, manner of speaking and
moving, even, perhaps, his attractive wife and the whole social-
cultural aura that surrounded the Kennedy Administration, all
contributed to the style. But, although it is important to realize that
many factors influence the audience's perception and identification
of style, certainly understanding the choice of language and the way
it is used is central to the development of a rhetorical perspective.

All language has some emotive content that varies in intensity
according to the audience and the situation. The semantic value of
words, for example, could vary with experience so that mentioning a
"camp" would produce different reactions in the man
who remembers with pleasure a childhood experience from those
produced in the Jewish refugee who spent years in a German
concentration camp. Furthermore, our culture establishes and
develops certain values that are reflected in the impact language has
on hearers. "Free enterprise" was for a long time, and probably still
is for most Americans, a positive concept, and the use of the term

produced positive reactions, whereas "socialism" had the reverse impact. So that labeling a proposition as "socialistic," by the very act of applying that particular language, was likely to elicit negative responses. In arguments raging over Medicare, for example, there were those who dismissed the concept with the single "argument" that it was "socialized medicine." This points to a very important consideration in the rhetorical use of language: Language may be used as a *substitute* for other evidence. If a new school program, for example, was devised on an experimental basis, those who favored it and those who opposed it might well develop their principal rhetorical strategy by a careful choice of language rather than through a careful scrutiny of the evidence. One can easily imagine the proponents asserting that the experimental program was "innovative" (and therefore good) and critics denouncing the use of their children as "guinea pigs" (a bad way to treat children).

Any discussion of style usually touches on two elements of style that are of great importance: clarity and appropriateness. It can readily be seen that clarity is an important function of most rhetorical style. It is difficult to imagine being persuaded to agree to something if you did not understand what was expected of you. It must be said, of course, that in such areas as politics and international diplomacy there is sometimes virtue in ambiguity, or at least the speakers do not wish to confine or commit themselves to concrete action and prefer to offer vague generalizations of policy. Such a strategy may leave more options open to the speaker, but it cannot, in the long run, provide a clear persuasive direction. A professor once told his class that he demanded clarity first in all writing assignments; when he was jokingly asked if he preferred clarity to accuracy he replied "yes" immediately. For, as he explained, he could detect inaccuracy if the writer was clear, but the accuracy of a muddled presentation was difficult to judge. Rhetorical style should always place a high premium on clarity so that both the speaker and the audience can more readily judge precisely what is going on.

The needs of the audience and the occasion influence the appropriateness of the style. The President of the United States gives a formal address in formal language when advising the Congress of the State of the Union; he uses much less formal language when talking with a visiting group of Boy Scouts in the Rose Garden or when chatting with soldiers in a veterans hospital. Mr. Rudd's language choice, mentioned earlier, fit the circumstances under which it was used much more than it would if used during a debate of the Columbia University Senate.

It may have become apparent to the reader that style is intimately involved with ethos. When a speaker uses words in a particular way it influences our judgment of him. If he talks about police as "pigs," we react to a whole set of values and ideas that this linguistic choice represents. If a speaker is confused and unclear, we are likely to believe that he does not know what he is talking about. If a speaker behaves in a way we deem to be inappropriate, we are embarrassed or annoyed or even amused; we do not generally consider that such action represents a man of sense and judgment.

Style has been said to *be* the man. Certainly it is the culminating and integrating aspect of rhetorical behavior.

The speaker   The speaker's style is consistent with his purpose, his own image, and his knowledge of the audience. He is faced with choices. These choices, in stylistic matters as in all others, are determined by the speaker's view of his audience. The speaker considers his goals. If he wishes to influence a noncommitted audience, rather than move those who already agree with him, he must recognize the linguistic prejudices and potentials of that audience. For some audiences he would find that simply using the word "commune" would be sufficient to produce strong negative reactions before he had even the opportunity to describe the aims and attitudes of those who participated. An understanding of the relationship between ethos and style should help to guide the speaker as he selects language that affects the audience's reactions.

In order to make reasonable decisions the speaker must understand what the audience knows. He must estimate the feelings of the audience, and know enough of them to predict their emotional reactions to language. As he chooses language that is clear and vivid his yardstick is the meaningfulness of such choices to the audience.

The critic   The critic examines style for what it tells him of the speaker's ability and view of the world. The thoughtful critic can discern from style the speaker's values and the network of his ideas. For example, a speaker who uses a code phrase such as "law and order" is signaling a whole series of attitudes and values that the critic should explore. From the speaker's language choice, the critic, in effect, hypothesizes a whole world view that helps the critic understand the speaker's motivations and ultimate aims. Language choice that a speaker makes consistently may also indicate his belief in the efficacy of such a choice, and this would lead the critic to make inferences concerning the speaker's perception of his audience and their world-view. Essentially, the critic searches for the forces—motivations, emotions—at work through the language.

But perhaps the critic's most difficult task is to discover and to speculate about the relationships between style and other factors. For style, as the integrative rhetorical feature, leads the critic to attempt finally to distinguish and to identify the underlying rhetorical power of public discourse.

It has been the purpose of this chapter to explore the principles that underlie rhetorical activity, to establish a number of points from which the process of public communication can be viewed—in short, to contribute to the development of a rhetorical perspective.

The speaker can consider these principles as he prepares himself to attempt to influence audiences, and the critic can consider them as he is exposed to public discourse. All of what can be said about the rationale for public discourse cannot be said in one simple chapter; but the outlines for understanding the rhetorical process have, hopefully, been drawn. The essays that precede the speeches in this book afford examples of how the critic might employ the basic principles to examine rhetorical works. The speeches themselves offer the student the opportunity to study with great care and deliberation the persuasive process as it has operated and is operating.

PART TWO:

**Speeches
for Analysis
and Criticism**

3

The Primacy
of the Audience

CRITICAL INTRODUCTION

**Peace Among Ourselves:
Lincoln, King, and the
Rhetoric of Unity**

Almost a century separates Lincoln's Second Inaugural
Address and Martin Luther King's speech to the crowds assembled
for the March on Washington for Jobs and Freedom. Yet both strike
similar themes in their attempts to move a wide and varied audience.

Lincoln, the war leader, facing a still-divided nation at war with
itself, sensed the rhetorical problems facing him and sought to
articulate for his divergent listeners the guiding philosophy for a
nation rent by suffering and soon to face the hard trials of a dearly
bought peace. "That rail-splitting lawyer is one of the wonders of
the day," the urbane Charles Francis Adams, Jr., wrote to his father.
Extolling Lincoln's "capacity for rising to the demands of the hour,"
Adams observed: "This inaugural strikes me in its grand simplicity
and directness as being for all time the historical keynote of this war;
in it a people seemed to speak in the sublimely simple utterance of
ruder times." [1] It was a time to speak for and to the people, and
Lincoln seized the day.

Lincoln began by dismissing the need for an extended speech

[1] Cited by Carl Sandburg, *Abraham Lincoln: The War Years,* New York:
Harcourt Brace Jovanovich, 1939, vol. IV, pp. 95–96.

detailing specifics of policy and action. It was true that all during the course of the war "public declarations had been constantly called forth on every point and phase of the great contest," and the audience was not expected to demand a long recitation of the facts relating to the progress of the war. Lincoln's brief account of the immediate events surrounding the commencement of hostilities merely reminded the northern listeners that the war was forced on the federal government and the people of the North who would not let the nation "perish"—a short, reinforcing statement of justification quite in line with prevailing northern opinion. As Lincoln moved to a discussion of the "peculiar and powerful interest," the colored slaves of the South, he subtly reinterpreted the war's underlying cause in a simple, moral cast: "All knew that this interest was somehow the cause of the war." Even though Lincoln immediately asserted that "the Government claimed no right to do more than to restrict the territorial enlargement of it," the suggestion that the war was rooted in the moral question of human slavery was firmly planted. Even though it was evident in 1860 that the question was the rock upon which the Union might founder, Lincoln's First Inaugural was a more decidedly legal investigation of the constitutional and political problems and evidenced a clear attempt on Lincoln's part to disassociate himself from the Abolitionist image of him conjured up in the South.[2] Abolitionism, indeed, was not popular in the North at the commencement of the war. Yet now Lincoln, with his statement that the "cause of the conflict" had ceased "before the conflict itself," clearly alluded to the Emancipation Proclamation and clearly put the basis of the war on a high moral, rather than political, plane.

To substantiate the purity of northern motives, the President proceeded to appeal to the generally accepted belief in divine intervention in the affairs of men. Each side, Lincoln pointed out, had invoked God's aid against the other. Yet it was strange to him that "any men should dare to ask a just God's assistance in wringing their bread from the sweat of other men's faces," and his humble admonition that he and his audience should "judge not, that we be not judged," does not diminish the impact of Lincoln's statement.

[2] For an excellent analysis of Lincoln's First Inaugural see Marie Hochmuth Nicholas, "Lincoln's First Inaugural Address," in J. Jeffery Auer, ed., *Antislavery and Disunion, 1858–1861*, New York: Harper & Row, 1963, pp. 392–414.

American slavery is clearly an offence, and, if God wills it, the war will continue until "all the wealth piled by the bondsman's two hundred and fifty years of unrequited toil shall be sunk, and until every drop of blood drawn with the lash shall be paid by another drawn with the sword." "The judgments of the Lord are true and righteous altogether"; the outcome was in the hands of the Almighty, and surely God would support the right. Because the collapse of the South, in spite of Lincoln's hesitancy in making outright predictions, was patently inevitable, the victory could be seen by the audience as divine patronage of the just cause. Such events as the draft riots in New York, the confusions over attitudes and actions toward runaway slaves, the debate and hesitancy preceding the promulgation of the Emancipation Proclamation, the cautious and limited tone of the Proclamation itself, all pointed to political perils and uncertainties associated with strongly allying the freedom of the slaves with the aims of the war. Now, however, with victory in sight, Lincoln attempted to direct his audience to the problem of Negro bondage and to enlist their emotional attachment toward the righteous cause of black freedom as cause and culmination of the conflict.

If the North could be united in terms of strong moral principle, if the war was a holy crusade for justice that was about to end in triumph, what implications did this have for a greater unity, a unity that encompassed the vanquished as well as the victors? Such a question leads to interesting speculation as to creation of a new rhetorical climate to be developed with the end of the war. It is clear from the tone and wording of Lincoln's justly famous closing paragraph that the audience was enjoined to eschew malice toward the defeated South, to offer instead charity, and to bind up wounds and not exacerbate them through vengeance and recrimination. If the audience was, indeed, convinced that the cause for the war had already been removed, that the right had already prevailed, then the cessation of hostilities would be the occasion for establishing a "just and lasting peace among ourselves." If the South accepted, as it must, the end of slavery, then the paramount political task became one of promoting the process of healing and not of prescribing the methods of punishment.

As has been argued earlier, persuasion is not usually the result of one speech. A variety of messages, experiences, pressures, and perceptions shape the actions of audiences. And it is evident that Lincoln's seeming vision of the best paths to reconstruction of the union did not materialize; the Inaugural did not and could not insure that. But it does seem reasonable to conclude that it evidenced an attempt on Lincoln's part to establish, or begin to establish, a rhetorical climate that would promote unity and smooth the rough places of transition.

Unlike President Lincoln, Martin Luther King could not conclude that the cause of his struggle had been eliminated. A century of experience had shown that the end of slavery did not end the problems of the black man in America. Racial prejudice and discrimination had spawned an era of fear and frustration, of injustice and inhumanity culminating in either resignation or desperation on the part of blacks, and hostility or concern on the part of whites.

Nevertheless, with Lincoln, King had a vision of unity erected on accepted, cherished values. As he stood on the steps of the Memorial looking over the vast crowds spread out before him, in the "symbolic shadow" of Lincoln, Dr. King directly and stylistically conjured up the spirit of past American promise of freedom as he referred to the signing of the Emancipation Proclamation, "Five score years ago." King's dream, as he asserted in his speech, was "deeply rooted in the American dream." As fundamentally concerned with the plight of the black man as King's speech is, it evidences a strong attempt to interpret black aspirations in the context of the American tradition, a tradition shared and presumably valued not only by the throngs assembled before him but also by those who watched the proceedings on television, and by the men and women charged with the responsibility of governing the country—those who had to act on the civil rights legislation then being considered by Congress.

King's historical and traditional appeal to American values of justice and equality is paramount throughout the speech.[3] The very "hallowed spot" upon which he stood was made so by the symbolic presence of Lincoln. The audience is reminded of the doctrines of "nullification and interposition," supposedly resolved and rejected as an outcome of the Civil War, still finding voice through the governor of Alabama. He asserted that, "if America is to be a great nation," then "all of God's children will be able to sing with new

[3] Compare King's perception of the place of the black man in the American tradition with Malcolm X's position as stated in "The Ballot or the Bullet," pp. 135–153.

meaning—'my country 'tis of thee; sweet land of liberty; of thee I sing; land where my fathers died, land of the pilgrim's pride; from every mountainside, let freedom ring.' " It is within this context of a shared historical tradition that King appealed to his audience.

King's appeals, however, were firmly based in the conviction that, although the tradition is shared, the fruits of the American tree of liberty are decidedly not. Black Americans live "on a lonely island of poverty in the midst of a vast ocean of material prosperity." The blessings of the American experience have become a reality for most whites, but for blacks they remain at best a hope, a "dream" still. The practices rather than the promises of America had produced disunity and discord, and King was quick to point out that they would continue to do so. "It would be fatal," King maintained, "for the nation to overlook the urgency of the movement and to underestimate the determination of the Negro." The nation cannot return to "business as usual. There will be neither rest nor tranquility in America until the Negro is granted his citizenship rights." King predicted the continuance of the "whirlwinds of revolt" until the "bright day of justice emerges." To those who call for order, stability, and civil peace, King countered with the appeal to justice. But the implied threat is clearly countered and softened with a direct appeal for moderation: "In the process of gaining our rightful place we must not be guilty of wrongful deeds."

Imbedded within his appeal to unity among all Americans in the fulfillment of the American promise is King's plea for unity and focus within the movement. The strategy of demonstration and civil disobedience had brought to blacks and to those whites who joined them an awareness of their own ability to dramatize long-hidden problems, and a sense of the potential for change through confrontation. Many in the Washington audience were veterans of sit-ins, marches, and arrest. They had been set on by dogs, sprayed with high-power water hoses, thrown in jail. King's nonviolent philosophy had been sorely tested in the crucible of protest. He sought a unity based on "creative protest" and cautioned that it must not be allowed to degenerate into physical violence. "Again and again we must rise to the majestic heights of meeting physical force with soul force."

King's philosophy of confrontation, depending as it did on "dramatizing a shameful condition"—that is, on bringing white Americans and the white American power structure face to face with those conditions and realities that should shame them—led him

naturally to promote a strong sense of racial unity. Racial unity
within the movement itself, of course, was particularly essential
from King's point of view. As is obvious, King did not advocate or
contemplate the violent destruction of American institutions, but,
rather, he wished American institutions to live up to American
ideals. The black was "an exile in his own land," who should no
longer be compelled to "languish in the corners of American
society." If such an aim was to be accomplished, and accomplished
nonviolently, whites as well as blacks had to work in cooperation.
King hoped to convince his white listeners that "their freedom is
inextricably bound to our freedom," and he cautioned blacks that
the "marvelous new militancy . . . must not lead us to a distrust of
all white people." He spoke of "white brothers" who were present in
his audience that day, and argued that the "battlements of injustice"
could only be carried by a "biracial army." The need for a black-
white alliance he summed up simply: "We cannot walk alone." [4]
Only through racial unity within the movement, King argued, could
victory be achieved. His final words to the audience reinforced his
belief that "black men and white men, Jews and Gentiles, Catholics
and Protestants," would finally join hands to celebrate freedom.

The March on Washington was a kind of emotional climax for the
early civil rights movement. Those who had been struggling and
suffering in various parts of the country were brought together in
one place, where they observed, participated in, and began to
understand the dimensions of a growing mass movement. Surely
among the black laborers from the rural South, the aggressive,
dedicated organizers of the Student Nonviolent Coordinating
Committee, the white liberals from the universities, the labor
leaders, the ghetto-dwellers from the North, the quiet, committed
Quakers, the religious leaders of a variety of faiths, among these
different groups were different perceptions about the nature of the
movement and about its aims. Martin Luther King was, as Louis
Lomax wrote, "to the Negro revolt as Paul was to the early church;
not only does he go from town to town inspiring Negroes to take

[4] For an account of King's difficulty with black power advocates who
questioned King's philosophy and tactics, see Robert L. Scott and Wayne
Brockriede, *The Rhetoric of Black Power*, New York: Harper & Row, 1969,
especially Scott's essays, "Justifying Violence: The Rhetoric of Militant Black
Power," pp. 132–145, and "Black Power Bends Martin Luther King," pp.
166–177.

action, but he returns to suffer with them in time of trouble"; [5] he
was the voice and spirit of the movement. In this speech he sought
to give a focus, a unity of purpose to those who struggled in
different ways and in different places for justice for the black man.
King articulated both the immediate legislative aims and the
long-term goals upon which adherents to the cause could coalesce.
"We will not be satisfied," he said, "until justice rolls down like
waters and righteousness like a mighty stream." And justice, for
King, involved some very specific things. His reference to the
inability of blacks to find "lodging in the motels of the highways
and the hotels of the cities," and his allusion to the degrading "for
whites only" signs, directly refer to abuses dealt with in the
proposed Civil Rights Act. Accordingly, on the level of immediate
action, lobbying for the passage of the Act was set forth as a clear
and concrete goal. The restrictions on the voting rights of blacks was
another specific problem that might be ameliorated through direct
legislative action. But King knew and sought to focus unified effort
toward solving problems more deepseated than those that could be
resolved through immediate legislative relief. In the early moments
of his speech, King contrasted the "poverty" of the black with the
"material prosperity" of the rest of the nation. And later he asserted
that "We cannot be satisfied as long as . . . a Negro in New York
believes he has nothing for which to vote." Freedom and justice for
King included the right of the black man to enjoy his honestly
earned portion of the wealth of this wealthy nation. It is true,
however, that King did not devote much of his speech to the
economic problems of blacks. Much relating to the black man's right
to share in America's prosperity is implied in King's concept of
freedom, and this speech tries to put the problem in the framework
of the larger, shared American values. The words "freedom" and
"justice" abound in the text, and obviously are prerequisite to full
material prosperity in King's thinking.

But King was sounding a note more than he was prescribing a
detailed program. As the very soul and prophet of the blossoming
civil rights movement, King was expected to set the tone. Like
Lincoln's inaugural, King's speech points toward the creation of a
rhetorical climate in which his supporters in the audience could
interpret and rationalize their actions, and which, if firmly
established, could move the entire civil rights debate into the area of

[5] Louis E. Lomax, *The Negro Revolt,* New York: Harper & Row, 1962, p.
103.

accepted American values rather than what would pacify, or "satisfy," the black man. Only when the struggle was viewed as one to "make real the promises of democracy" could the argument for a "cooling off" period embodied in the "tranquilizing drug of gradualism" be rejected out of hand.

Both Lincoln and King had a vision of unity firmly based on values professed by their audiences. Theirs were attempts, by identifying with ideals commonly held to be consistent with the highest aspirations of American society, to build a rhetorical universe in which arguments and actions could be measured against what was morally right. These were lofty aspirations. Neither succeeded in the time allotted to each of them in restricting and directing the course of the rhetorical stream as each would have wished. The "bitterness and hatred" that King abhorred and the malice that Lincoln hoped to avoid were and are all too evident. But both speeches stand as testaments to unity and harmony, as antidotes in the historical consciousness of the American people against the poisons of divisiveness and discord. They show a keen awareness of rhetorical needs and situations and are exemplary efforts to shape events through appeals to deeply planted audience values.

ABRAHAM LINCOLN

SECOND INAUGURAL ADDRESS

Fellow-countrymen, at this second appearing to take the oath of the presidential office there is less occasion for an extended address than there was at the first. Then a statement somewhat in detail of a course to be pursued seemed fitting and proper. Now, at the expiration of four years, during which public declarations have been constantly called forth on every point and phase of the great contest which still absorbs the attention and engrosses the energies of the nation, little that is new could be presented. The progress of

Abraham Lincoln's speech was given in Washington, D.C., on March 4, 1865. It is reprinted from *Inaugural Addresses of the Presidents of the United States,* Washington, D.C.: GPO, 1961, pp. 127–128.

our arms, upon which all else chiefly depends, is as well known to the public as to myself, and it is, I trust, reasonably satisfactory and encouraging to all. With high hope for the future, no prediction in regard to it is ventured.

On the occasion corresponding to this four years ago all thoughts were anxiously directed to an impending civil war. All dreaded it, all sought to avert it. While the inaugural address was being delivered from this place, devoted altogether to *saving* the Union without war, insurgent agents were in the city seeking to *destroy* it without war—seeking to dissolve the Union and divide effects by negotiation. Both parties deprecated war, but one of them would *make* war rather than let the nation survive, and the other would *accept* war rather than let it perish, and the war came.

One-eighth of the whole population was colored slaves, not distributed generally over the Union, but localized in the southern part of it. These slaves constituted a peculiar and powerful interest. All knew that this interest was somehow the cause of the war. To strengthen, perpetuate, and extend this interest was the object for which the insurgents would rend the Union even by war, while the Government claimed no right to do more than to restrict the territorial enlargement of it. Neither party expected for the war the magnitude or the duration which it has already attained. Neither anticipated that the *cause* of the conflict might cease with or even before the conflict itself should cease. Each looked for an easier triumph, and a result less fundamental and astounding. Both read the same Bible and pray to the same God, and each invokes His aid against the other. It may seem strange that any men should dare to ask a just God's assistance in wringing their bread from the sweat of other men's faces, but let us judge not, that we be not judged. The prayers of both could not be answered. That of neither has been answered fully. The Almighty has His own purposes. "Woe unto the world because of offenses; for it must needs be that offenses come, but woe to that man by whom the offense cometh." If we shall suppose that American slavery is one of those offenses which, in the providence of God, must needs come, but which, having continued through His appointed time, He now wills to remove, and that He gives to both North and South this terrible war as the woe due to those by whom the offense came, shall we discern therein any departure from those divine attributes which the believers in a living God always ascribe to Him? Fondly do we hope, fervently do we pray, that this mighty scourge of war may speedily pass away. Yet, if

God wills that it continue until all the wealth piled by the bondsman's two hundred and fifty years of unrequited toil shall be sunk,
and until every drop of blood drawn with the lash shall be paid by
another drawn with the sword, as was said three thousand years ago,
so still it must be said, "The judgments of the Lord are true and
righteous altogether."

With malice toward none, with charity for all, with firmness in the
right as God gives us to see the right, let us strive on to finish the
work we are in, to bind up the nation's wounds, to care for him who
shall have borne the battle and for his widow and his orphan, to do
all which may achieve and cherish a just and lasting peace among
ourselves and with all nations.

MARTIN LUTHER KING, Jr.

I HAVE A DREAM

Five score years ago, a great American, in whose symbolic
shadow we stand today, signed the Emancipation Proclamation. This
momentous decree came as a great beacon of light and of hope to
millions of Negro slaves who had been seared in the flames of
withering injustice. It came as a joyous daybreak to end the long
night of their captivity.

But one hundred years later, the Negro still is not free. One
hundred years later, the life of the Negro is still sadly crippled by the
manacles of segregation and the chains of discrimination.

One hundred years later, the Negro lives on a lonely island of
poverty in the midst of a vast ocean of material prosperity. One
hundred years later, the Negro is still languished in the corners of
American society and finds himself an exile in his own land. So we
have come here today to dramatize a shameful condition.

In a sense we have come to our nation's capital to cash a check.
When the architects of our republic wrote the magnificent words of
the Constitution and the Declaration of Independence, they were
signing a promissory note to which every American was to fall heir.

Martin Luther King's speech was given in Washington, D.C., on August 28,
1963. It is reprinted by permission from Roy L. Hill, ed., Denver: Golden Bell,
Press, 1964, pp. 371–375.

This note was a promise that all men, yes, black men as well as white men, would be granted the unalienable rights of life, liberty, and the pursuit of happiness.

It is obvious today that America has defaulted on this promissory note insofar as her citizens of color are concerned. Instead of honoring this sacred obligation, America has given the Negro people a bad check; which has come back marked "insufficient funds."

But we refuse to believe that the bank of justice is bankrupt. We refuse to believe that there are insufficient funds in the great vaults of opportunity of this nation. So we have come to cash this check—a check that will give us upon demand the riches of freedom and the security of justice.

We have also come to this hallowed spot to remind America of the *Justice now* fierce urgency of now. This is no time to engage in the luxury of cooling off or to take the tranquilizing drug of gradualism. Now is the time to make real the promises of democracy. Now is the time to rise from the dark and desolate valley of segregation to the sunlit path of racial justice. Now is the time to lift our nation from the quicksands of racial injustice to the solid rock of brotherhood. Now is the time to make justice a reality for all of God's children.

It would be fatal for the nation to overlook the urgency of the movement and to underestimate the determination of the Negro. This sweltering summer of the Negro's legitimate discontent will not pass until there is an invigorating autumn of freedom and equality. 1963 is not an end but a beginning. Those who hope that the Negro needed to blow off steam and will now be content will have a rude awakening if the nation returns to business as usual.

There will be neither rest nor tranquility in America until the Negro is granted his citzenship rights. The whirlwinds of revolt will continue to shake the foundations of our nation until the bright day of justice emerges.

But there is something that I must say to my people who stand on the warm threshold which leads into the palace of justice. In the process of gaining our rightful place we must not be guilty of wrongful deeds.

Let us not seek to satisfy our thirst for freedom by drinking from the cup of bitterness and hatred. We must forever conduct our struggle on the high plane of dignity and discipline. We must not allow our creative protest to degenerate into physical violence. Again and again we must rise to the majestic heights of meeting physical force with soul force.

The marvelous new militancy which has engulfed the Negro

community must not lead us to a distrust of all white people, for many of our white brothers, as evidenced by their presence here today, have come to realize that their destiny is tied up with our destiny and they have come to realize that their freedom is inextricably bound to our freedom. This offense we share mounted to storm the battlements of injustice must be carried forth by a bi-racial army. We cannot walk alone.

And as we walk, we must make the pledge that we shall always march ahead. We cannot turn back. There are those who are asking the devotees of civil rights, "When will you be satisfied?" We can never be satisfied as long as the Negro is the victim of the unspeakable horrors of police brutality.

We can never be satisfied as long as our bodies, heavy with the fatigue of travel, cannot gain lodging in the motels of the highways and the hotels of the cities. We cannot be satisfied as long as the Negro's basic mobility is from a smaller ghetto to a larger one.

We can never be satisfied as long as our children are stripped of their selfhood and robbed of their dignity by signs stating "for whites only." We cannot be satisfied as long as a Negro in Mississippi cannot vote and a Negro in New York believes he has nothing for which to vote. No, we are not satisfied, and we will not be satisfied until justice rolls down like waters and righteousness like a mighty stream.

I am not unmindful that some of you have come here out of excessive trials and tribulation. Some of you have come fresh from narrow jail cells. Some of you have come from areas where your quest for freedom left you battered by the storms of persecution and staggered by the winds of police brutality. You have been the veterans of creative suffering. Continue to work with the faith that unearned suffering is redemptive.

Go back to Mississippi; go back to Alabama; go back to South Carolina; go back to Georgia; go back to Louisiana; go back to the slums and ghettos of the Northern cities, knowing that somehow this situation can, and will be changed. Let us not wallow in the valley of despair.

So I say to you, my friends, that even though we must face the difficulties of today and tomorrow, I still have a dream. It is a dream deeply rooted in the American dream that one day this nation will rise up and live out the true meaning of its creed—we hold these truths to be self evident, that all men are created equal.

I have a dream that one day on the red hills of Georgia, sons of former slaves and sons of former slave-owners will be able to sit down together at the table of brotherhood.

I have a dream that one day, even the state of Mississippi, a state sweltering with the heat of injustice, sweltering with the heat of oppression, will be transformed into an oasis of freedom and justice.

I have a dream my four little children will one day live in a nation where they will not be judged by the color of their skin but by the content of their character. I have a dream today!

I have a dream that one day, down in Alabama, with its vicious racists, with its governor having his lips dripping with the words of interposition and nullification, that one day, right there in Alabama, little black boys and black girls will be able to join hands with little white boys and white girls as sisters and brothers. I have a dream today!

I have a dream that one day every valley shall be exalted, every hill and mountain shall be made low, the rough places shall be made plain, and the crooked places shall be made straight and the glory of the Lord will be revealed and all flesh shall see it together.

This is our hope. This is the faith that I go back to the South with.

With this faith we will be able to hew out of the mountain of despair a stone of hope. With this faith we will be able to transform the jangling discords of our nation into a beautiful symphony of brotherhood.

With this faith we will be able to work together, to pray together, to struggle together, to go to jail together, to stand up for freedom together, knowing that we will be free one day. This will be the day when all of God's children will be able to sing with new meaning— "my country 'tis of thee; sweet land of liberty; of thee I sing; land where my fathers died, land of the pilgrim's pride; from every mountain side, let freedom ring"—and if America is to be a great nation, this must become true.

So let freedom ring from the prodigious hilltops of New Hampshire.

Let freedom ring from the mighty mountains of New York.

Let freedom ring from the heightening Alleghenies of Pennsylvania.

Let freedom ring from the snow-capped Rockies of Colorado.

Let freedom ring from the curvaceous slopes of California.
But not only that.
Let freedom ring from Stone Mountain of Georgia.
Let freedom ring from Lookout Mountain of Tennessee.
Let freedom ring from every hill and molehill of Mississippi, from every mountainside, let freedom ring.

And when we allow freedom to ring, when we let it ring from every village and hamlet, from every state and city, we will be able to speed up that day when all of God's children—black men and white men, Jews and Gentiles, Catholics and Protestants—will be able to join hands and to sing in the words of the old Negro spiritual. "Free at last, free at last; thank God Almighty, we are free at last."

4

Identification: The Audience and the Topic

CRITICAL INTRODUCTION

Seeking Old and Precious Moral Values: Bright and Roosevelt Redefine the Topic

In their efforts to promote identification between the audience and the topic, John Bright's short, striking antiwar speech, "The Angel of Death," and President Franklin D. Roosevelt's First Inaugural demonstrate an interesting similarity. Addressing themselves to profound national problems in a time of distress, both speakers sought to shift the focus of the controversy over appropriate courses of action and points of emphasis. With a strong emotional base in very real and affecting difficulties, both identified their vision with cultural values.

In 1855, when John Bright rose to address the House of Commons, Great Britain was at war with Russia. The battleground was the Crimea. Although the British had not suffered any serious military reverses, tales of inept leadership and incredible hardship and suffering had filtered back to England. The country had been at peace for a generation before the outbreak of the conflict, and, while the initial patriotic impulse had excited the people and government alike with dreams of martial glory and adventure, the growing casualty lists had both saddened and sobered the country.

Bright and a hardy band of colleagues had vigorously but vainly opposed the war. For their opposition, the pacifists had been the object of severe attack and ridicule. In spite of this, John Bright, a powerful and respected speaker, had managed to retain in the House of Commons an audience that would listen to, if not act positively on, what he had to say.

Bright sought identification with the topic under discussion in two ways. First, he hoped to deemphasize the political aspects of the war controversy, and, second, to stress the morality and nobility of ending bloodshed.

It is immediately clear that Bright did not wish to speak as an opponent of the Government. His feeling of the general uneasiness about the news from the East, the theater of military operations, was gained, in part, by "speaking to Gentlemen who sit on either side of this House." That is, by speaking to both Government and opposition supporters, because the two groups sat facing each other in the chambers of the House of Commons. This speech, Bright implied, was not to be one of attack on his political enemies, but rather, one that voiced common concerns. He early pointed out the relevance of the question to all classes of his countrymen: to the inhabitants of "the castle of the noble, the mansion of the wealthy, and the cottage of the poor and the lowly." Bright made his appeal "on behalf of all these classes."

A major passage of the speech was directed toward his long-time political foe Lord Palmerston, the Prime Minister. This personal reference reinforced Bright's nonpolitical stance. For, if Palmerston would "honestly and frankly . . . endeavour . . . to put an end to this war," then Bright promised that "no word of mine, no vote of mine, will be given to shake his power for one single moment, or to change his position in this House." Bright's entreaty directed at Palmerston is interlaced with his strong call for a higher moral criterion for judging political actions. This moral theme began earlier in the speech and was brought to a climax in the appeal to Palmerston.

At the outset, Bright demonstrated his primary concern, a concern that went beyond patriotism or purely national political goals. The disquiet in the country that Bright described stemmed from human rather than national interests. He readily dismissed the consequences of the fighting as he asserted that "I do not suppose that your troops are to be beaten in actual conflict with the foe, or that they will be driven into the sea." A battle won or lost was of relative unimportance when compared with the higher value of human life. The clash of arms may have various outcomes, but to Bright the obviously overriding one was that "many homes in England in which there now exists a fond hope that the distant one may return . . . may be rendered desolate when the next mail shall arrive." Victory, the traditional touchstone of patriotism, seemed of little consequence to Bright when contrasted with the human price.

Bright was relentless in his goal of identifying the whole question of the war with the preservation of life. Bright's powerful and guiding metaphor is the biblical one. The remorseless slaying did not even allow for the exceptions granted to the ancient Jews in Egypt; it was arbitrary and inevitable, striking all men of all classes: "The Angel of Death is abroad throughout the land; you may almost hear the beating of his wings. There is no one, as when the first-born were slain of old, to sprinkle with blood the lintel and the two side-posts of our doors, that he may spare and pass on." At Palmerston, and through him his supporters and the proponents of the war, Bright directed a plea that was meant to go beyond the walls of Parliament to the wider audience. Palmerston was urged to cap his long career with actions leading to peace, a course that "cannot be but a source of gratification to him." War and peace are finally contrasted as Bright describes what the Prime Minister could achieve. By returning the sword to the scabbard, Bright argued, Palmerston would restore tranquility, he would have "saved his country." And this outcome is in marked contrast with the "torrents of blood," and the "indescribable calamities of war."

Bright did not mention in this speech what might be called "war aims." For against what might be presumed by some to be the public good, Bright set personal loss. Identification was not sought in terms of what may or may not be gained by fighting but, rather, identification was sought through appeal to a most basic human motivation, the preservation of human life. Upon that strong motivational base, Bright implied the immorality of the destructiveness of war. By not dealing with political questions, Bright set up a clear polarity between war and peace that is as between good and evil, inviting the audience to identify with the good.

Franklin Roosevelt assumed the Presidency at a time of profound crisis for the American people. Widespread unemployment, bank failures, mortgage foreclosures—the extensive economic disaster had seemed to the mass of the new President's audience to paralyze the will and frustrate the actions of government. Roosevelt's obvious goal was to bolster the morale and restore the confidence of the

people in the government's ability and desire to take decisive action
to reverse the grim trend. The topic under discussion was one that
touched all, but the President hoped to promote a different kind of
identification with the problems of the depression. Roosevelt's
strategy called for a sharp delineation of the major considerations of
policy and program cast in stern moral terms which pointed to the
unity and dedication that only a truly national effort could bring.

The implication was clear throughout the speech that material
difficulties resulted in part from moral lapses by those charged with
national responsibilities. The national "distress comes from no
failure of substance," Roosevelt asserted. "We are stricken with no
plague of locusts. . . . Nature still offers her bounty and human
efforts have multiplied it. Plenty is at our doorstep, but a generous
use of it languishes in the very sight of the supply." The cause of this
dreadful anomaly is clear: Roosevelt indicted the "practices of the
unscrupulous money changers" who had "failed through their own
stubbornness and their own incompetence." By charging that the
"false leadership" was motivated by "the lure of profit," and
directly condemning a "generation of self-seekers," the President
provided the moral antithesis against which to judge the new
leadership. With the defeat of "The money changers [who] have fled
from their high seats in the temple of our civilization," it was now
possible for the new Administration to "restore that temple to the
ancient truths." The country would now be set upon the proper
course if "social values more noble than mere monetary profit"
could be applied.

The ancient truths that stood in contrast to the "mad chase for
evanescent profits" and the "callous and selfish wrongdoing" were
those that promoted the realization that "our true destiny is not to
be ministered unto but to minister to ourselves and to our fellow-
men." Roosevelt enumerated the noble social values upon which he
launched his campaign against economic distress: "honesty . . .
honor . . . the sacredness of obligations . . . faithful protection . . .
unselfish performance." The moral tone of a national crusade was
clearly set.

On this firm moral foundation President Roosevelt attempted to
build a new identification between the audience and the problems of
the depression. The guiding and consistent metaphor throughout the
speech is one of war. Given the emphasis on the moral code
underlying the attack on material distress, the war becomes almost a

holy one; indeed, the President began his speech by calling
Inauguration Day "a day of national consecration." Even though
Roosevelt recognized that "restoration calls, however, not for
changes in ethics alone," the action for which the nation seemed to
yearn was decidedly prescribed within the framework of Roosevelt's
vision of moral regeneration: ". . . when there is no vision,"
Roosevelt asserted, "the people perish." The dimensions of
Roosevelt's moral vision were made abundantly clear in the opening
passages of the speech, and it is on the basis of this vision that the
"war" would be fought.

The multitude whom Roosevelt sought to influence and lead were
called upon to identify themselves with the soldier, emulating the
military virtues of sacrifice and courage. Only through the unity and
dedication that war brings could the common enemy be vanquished.
A close examination of the text reveals the pervasiveness of this
metaphor.

The "fear" that Roosevelt early identified as the principal enemy
was dangerous because it was responsible for paralyzing "needed
efforts to convert retreat into advance." Immediately the problem
was posed in terms of a military campaign, and support of the new
leadership called necessary for "victory." The metaphor became
explicit when Roosevelt recommended "treating the task as we
would treat the emergency of a war." In recognizing their "interdependence on each other," Americans "must move as a trained and
loyal army willing to sacrifice for the good of a common discipline,"
for "without such discipline . . . no leadership become effective."
Again and again Roosevelt returned to his call for warlike patriotic
dedication: ". . . the larger purpose will bind upon us all as a sacred
obligation with a unity of duty hitherto evoked only in time of
armed strife." The words "action" and "attack" appear frequently
throughout the speech, pointing up the martial character needed to
struggle against the massive economic distress and discontent.

No doubt placing the entire problem in this light was consistent
with Roosevelt's vision of the action he would take or consider in
the days ahead; the speech itself makes this evident. The outbreak of
war was not consistent with a prolonged national debate. When the
enemy had landed, terrorizing the countryside, protracted consideration of decisive measures could not be tolerated. Measures designed
to put people to work (partly by "direct recruiting by the government"), to "provide for a better use of the land," to prevent

foreclosures of homes and farms, to reduce the costs of government, to provide national planning for transportation, communications, and other public utilities, to supervise banking activities, to establish a sound currency—measures that seemed to call for the massive reorganization and redistribution of our resources, energies, and priorities would all have to be acted on quickly and without selfish, petty carping which delayed immediate action. The President argued that Americans must be "ready and willing to submit our lives and property to such discipline because it makes possible a leadership which aims at a larger good." Roosevelt assumed "the leadership of this great army of our people, dedicated to a disciplined attack upon our common problems."

If the audience saw the economic plight of the nation as a combat situation, if the President's effort to identify the problem in terms of a morally grounded war were successful, then the possibilities for decisive, and even unilateral Executive action could be contemplated. While he professed faith in the normal and orderly constitutional progress of government, Roosevelt's definition of and perspective on the topic enabled him to foreshadow the possibilities of stern and unusual presidential action. If the President should fail in his efforts to bring about the "speedy adoption" of corrective measures, if Congress should not pass legislation to remedy the problem, and if "the national emergency is still critical," the President would ask for broad (and here unspecified) power "to wage a war against the emergency as great as the power that would be given me if we were in fact invaded by a foreign foe." Undoubtedly, to Roosevelt's critics such a declaration (his enemies would have called it a threat) sounded ominous. But it grew out of and was buttressed by Roosevelt's attempts to promote a special identification between the audience and the topic.

In both the speeches that follow, then, may be seen the skilled use of audience values and emotions to promote the speaker's particular point of view toward the problem. Both afford examples in which the identification of the audience with the topic is promoted in a way consistent with the audience's accepted code of moral conduct and with the speaker's intentions.

JOHN BRIGHT

THE ANGEL OF DEATH

I am one of those forming the majority of the House, I
suspect, who are disposed to look upon our present position as one
of more than ordinary gravity. I am one, also, of those, not probably
constituting so great a majority of the House, who regret extremely
the circumstances which have obliged the right hon. Gentlemen who
are now upon this bench to secede from the Government of the
noble Lord the Member for Tiverton. I do not take upon me for a
moment to condemn them; because I think, if there be anything in
which a man must judge for himself, it is whether he should take
office if it be offered to him, whether he should secede from office,
whether he should serve under a particular leader, or engage in the
service of the Crown, or retain office in a particular emergency. In
such cases I think that the decision must be left to his own
conscience and his own judgment; and I should be the last person to
condemn any one for the decision to which he might come. I think,
however, that the speech of the right hon. Gentleman is one which
the House cannot have listened to without being convinced that he
and his retiring colleagues have been moved to the course which they
have taken by a deliberate judgment upon this question, which,
whether it be right or wrong, is fully explained, and is honest to the
House and to the country. Now, Sir, I said that I regretted their
secession, because I am one of those who do not wish to see the
Government of the noble Lord the Member for Tiverton overthrown. The House knows well, and nobody knows better than the
noble Lord, that I have never been one of his ardent and enthusiastic
supporters. I have disapproved much of his policy both at home and
abroad; but I hope that I do not bear to him, as I can honestly say
that I do not bear to any man in this House—for from all I have
received unnumbered courtesies—any feeling that takes even the
tinge of a personal animosity; and, even if I did, at a moment so
grave as this, no feeling of a personal character whatever should
prevent me from doing that which I think now, of all times, we are

John Bright's speech was given in the House of Commons, Westminster, on
February 23, 1855. It is reprinted from *Hansard's Parliamentary Debates,* 3d
series, CXXXVI (1855), cols. 1755–1762.

called upon to do—that which we honestly and conscientiously believe to be for the permanent interests of the country. We are in this position, that for a month past, at least, there has been a chaos in the regions of the Administration. Nothing can be more embarrassing—I had almost said nothing can be more humiliating—than the position which we offer to the country; and I am afraid that the knowledge of our position is not confined to the limits of these islands. It will be admitted that we want a Government; that if the country is to be saved from the breakers which now surround it, there must be a Government; and it devolves upon the House of Commons to rise to the gravity of the occasion, and to support any man who is conscious of his responsibility, and who is honestly offering and endeavouring to deliver the country from the embarrassment in which we now find it. We are at war, and I shall not say one single sentence with regard to the policy of the war or its origin, and I know not that I shall say a single sentence with regard to the conduct of it; but the fact is that we are at war with the greatest military Power, probably, of the world, and that we are carrying on our operations at a distance of 3,000 miles from home, and in the neighbourhood of the strongest fortifications of that great military empire. I will not stop to criticise—though it really invites me—the fact that some who have told us that we were in danger from the aggressions of that empire, at the same time told us that empire was powerless for aggression, and also that it was impregnable to attack. By some means, however, the public have been alarmed as if that aggressive power were unbounded, and they have been induced to undertake an expedition, as if the invasion of an impregnable country were a matter of holiday-making rather than of war. But we are now in a peculiar position with regard to that war; for, if I am not mistaken—and I think I gathered as much from the language of the right hon. Gentleman—at this very moment terms have been agreed upon—agreed upon by the Cabinet of Lord Aberdeen; consented to by the noble Lord the Member for Tiverton, when he was in that Cabinet; and ratified and confirmed by him upon the formation of his own Government—and that those terms are now specifically known and understood; and that they have been offered to the Government with which this country is at war, and in conjunction with France and Austria—one, certainly, and the other supposed to be, an ally of this country. Now, those terms consist of four propositions, which I shall neither describe nor discuss, because they are known to the House; but three of them are not matters of dispute; and, with

regard to the other, I think that the noble Lord the Member for the
City of London stated, upon a recent occasion, that it was involved
in these terms—that the preponderant power of Russia in the Black
Sea should cease, and that Russia had accepted it with that
interpretation. Therefore, whatever difference arises is merely as to
the mode in which that "preponderent power" shall be understood
or made to cease. Now, there are some Gentlemen not far from
me—there are men who write in the public press—there are
thousands of persons in the United Kingdom at this moment—and I
learn with astonishment and dismay that there are persons even in
that grave assembly which we are not allowed to specify by a name
in this House—who have entertained dreams—impracticable
theories—expectations of vast European and Asiatic changes, of
revived nationalities, and of a new map of Europe, if not of the
world, as a result or an object of this war. And it is from those
Gentlemen that we hear continually, addressed to the noble Lord
the Member for Tiverton, terms which I cannot well understand.
They call upon him to act, to carry on the war with vigour, and to
prosecute enterprises which neither his Government, nor any other
Government has ever seriously entertained; but I would appeal to
those Gentlemen whether it does not become us—regarding the true
interests and the true honour of the country—if our Government
have offered terms of peace to Russia, not to draw back from those
terms, not to cause any unnecessary delay, not to adopt any
subterfuge to prevent those terms being accepted, not to attempt
shuffles of any kind, not to endeavour to insist upon harder terms,
and thus make the approach of peace even still more distant than it
is at present? Whatever may be said about the honour of the country
in any other relation in regard to this affair, this, at least, I expect
every man who hears me to admit—that if terms of peace have been
offered they have been offered in good faith, and shall be in honour
and good faith adhered to; so that if, unfortunately for Europe and
humanity, there should be any failure at Vienna, no man should
point to the English Government and to the authorities and rulers of
this Christian country, and say that we have prolonged the war and
the infinite calamities of which it is the cause. Well, now, I said that
I was anxious that the Government of the noble Lord should not be
overthrown. Will the House allow me to say why I am so? The noble
Lord at the head of the Government has long been a great authority
with many persons in this country upon foreign policy. His late
colleague, and present envoy to Vienna, has long been a great
authority with a large portion of the people of this country upon

almost all political questions. With the exception of that unhappy selection of an ambassador at Constantinople, I hold that there are no men in this country more truly responsible for our present position in this war than the noble Lord who now fills the highest office in the State and the noble Lord who is now, I trust, rapidly approaching the scene of his labours in Vienna. ["Hear, hear!" *and cries of* "No, no!"] I do not say this now to throw blame upon those noble Lords, because their policy, which I hold to be wrong, they, without doubt, as firmly believe to be right; but I am only stating facts. It has been their policy that they have entered into war for certain objects, and I am sure that neither the noble Lord at the head of the Government nor his late colleague the noble Lord the Member for London will shrink from the responsibility which attaches to them. Well, Sir, now we have those noble Lords in a position which is, in my humble opinion, favourable to the termination of the troubles which exist. I think that the noble Lord at the head of the Government himself would have more influence in stilling whatever may exist of clamour in this country than any other Member of this House. I think, also, that the noble Lord the Member for London would not have undertaken the mission to Vienna if he had not entertained some strong belief that, by so doing, he might bring the war to an end. Nobody gains reputation by a failure in negotiation, and as that noble Lord is well acquainted with the whole question from beginning to end, I entertain a hope—I will not say a sanguine hope—that the result of that mission to Vienna will be to bring about a peace, to extricate this country from some of those difficulties inseparable from a state of war. There is one subject upon which I should like to put a question to the noble Lord at the head of the Government. I shall not say one word here about the state of the army in the Crimea, or one word about its numbers or its condition. Every Member of this House, every inhabitant of this country, has been sufficiently harrowed with details regarding it. To my solemn belief, thousands—nay, scores of thousands of persons—have retired to rest, night after night, whose slumbers have been disturbed, or whose dreams have been based upon the sufferings and agonies of our soldiers in the Crimea. I should like to ask the noble Lord at the head of the Government—although I am not sure if he will feel that he can or ought to answer the question—whether the noble Lord the Member for London has power, after discussions have commenced, and as soon as there shall be established good grounds for believing that the negotiations for the peace will prove successful, to enter into any armistice? ["No! no!" *and* "Hear, hear!"] I know not, Sir, who it is that says "No, no," but I should like to see any man get up and say that the destruction of 200,000 human lives lost on all sides during the course of this unhappy conflict is not a sufficient sacrifice. You are not pretending to conquer territory—you are not pretending to hold fortified or unfortified towns; you have offered terms of peace which, as I understand them, I do not say are not moderate; and breathes there a man in this House or in this country whose appetite for blood is so insatiable that, even when terms of peace have been offered and accepted, he pines for that assault in which of Russian, Turk, French, and English, as sure as one man dies, 20,000 corpses will strew the streets of Sebastopol? I say I should like to ask the noble Lord—and I am sure that he will feel, and that this House will feel, that I am speaking in no unfriendly manner towards the Government of which he is at the head—I should like to know, and I venture to hope that it is so, if the noble Lord the Member for London has power, at the earliest stage of these proceedings at Vienna, at which it can properly be done—and I should think that it might properly be done at a very early stage—to adopt a course by which all further waste of human life may be put an end to, and further animosity between three great nations be, as far as possible, prevented? I appeal to the noble Lord at the head of the Government and to this House; I am not now complaining of the war—I am not now complaining of the terms of peace, nor, indeed, of anything that has been done—but I wish to suggest to this House what, I believe, thousands, and tens of thousands, of the most educated and of the most Christian portion of the people of this country are feeling upon this subject, although, indeed, in the midst of a certain clamour in the country, they do not give public expression to their feelings. Your country is not in an advantageous state at this moment; from one end of the kingdom to the other there is a general collapse of industry. Those Members of this House not intimately acquainted with the trade and commerce of the country do not fully comprehend our position as to the diminution of employment and the lessening of wages. An increase in the cost of living is finding its way to the homes and hearts of a vast number of the labouring population. At the same time there is growing up—and, notwithstanding what some hon. Members of this House may think of me, no man regrets it more than I do—a bitter and angry feeling against that class which has for a long period conducted the public affairs of this country. I like political changes when such changes are made as the result, not of passion, but of deliberation and reason. Changes so made are safe, but changes made under the influence of violent exaggeration, or of the violent passions of public meetings, are not changes usually approved by this House or advantageous to the country. I cannot but notice, in speaking to Gentlemen who sit on either side of this House, or in speaking to anyone I meet between this House and any of those localities we frequent when this House is up—I cannot, I say, but notice that an uneasy feeling exists as to the news that may arrive by the very next mail from the East. I do not suppose that your troops are to be beaten in actual conflict with the foe, or that they will be driven into the sea; but I am certain that many homes in England in which there now exists a fond hope that the distant one may return—many such homes may be rendered desolate when the next mail shall arrive. The angel of death has been abroad throughout the land; you may almost hear the beating of his wings. There is no one, as when the first-born were slain of old, to sprinkle with blood the lintel and the two sideposts of our doors, that he may spare and pass on; he takes his victims from the castle of the noble, the mansion of the wealthy, and the cottage of the poor and the lowly, and it is on behalf of all these classes that I make this solemn appeal. I tell the noble Lord, that if he be ready honestly and frankly to endeavor, by the negotiations to be opened at Vienna, to put an end to this war, no word of mine, no vote of mine, will be given to shake his power for one single moment, or to change his position in this House. I am sure that the noble Lord is not inaccessible to appeals made to him from honest motives and with no unfriendly feeling. The noble Lord has been for more than forty years a Member of this House. Before I was born; he sat upon the Treasury bench, and he has devoted his life in the service of his country. He is no longer young, and his life has extended almost to the term allotted to man. I would ask, I would entreat the noble Lord to take a course which, when he looks back upon his whole political career—whatever he may therein find to be pleased with, whatever to regret—cannot but be a source of gratification to him. By adopting that course he would have the satisfaction of reflecting that, having obtained the object of his laudable ambition—having become the foremost subject of the Crown, the director of, it may be, the destinies of his country and the presiding genius in her councils—he had achieved a still higher and nobler ambition; that he had returned the sword to the scabbard—that at his word torrents of

blood had ceased to flow—that he had restored tranquillity to
Europe, and saved this country from the indescribable calamities of
war.

FRANKLIN D. ROOSEVELT

FIRST INAUGURAL ADDRESS

President Hoover, Mr. Chief Justice, my friends, this is a day
of national consecration, and I am certain that my fellow-Americans
expect that on my induction into the Presidency I will address them
with a candor and a decision which the present situation of our
nation impels.

This is preeminently the time to speak the truth, the whole truth,
frankly and boldly. Nor need we shrink from honestly facing
conditions in our country today. This great nation will endure as it
has endured, will revive and will prosper.

So first of all let me assert my firm belief that the only thing we
have to fear is fear itself—nameless, unreasoning, unjustified terror
which paralyzes needed efforts to convert retreat into advance.

In every dark hour of our national life a leadership of frankness
and vigor has met with that understanding and support of the people
themselves which is essential to victory. I am convinced that you will
again give that support to leadership in these critical days.

In such a spirit on my part and on yours we face our common
difficulties. They concern, thank God, only material things. Values
have shrunken to fantastic levels; taxes have risen; our ability to pay
has fallen; government of all kinds is faced by serious curtailment of
income; the means of exchange are frozen in the currents of trade;
the withered leaves of industrial enterprise lie on every side; farmers
find no markets for their produce; the savings of many years in
thousands of families are gone.

More important, a host of unemployed citizens face the grim
problem of existence, and an equally great number toil with little

Franklin D. Roosevelt's speech was given in Washington, D.C., on March 4,
1933. It is reprinted from *Inaugural Addresses of the Presidents of the United
States,* Washington, D.C.: GPO, 1961, pp. 235–239.

return. Only a foolish optimist can deny the dark realities of the
moment.

Yet our distress comes from no failure of substance. We are
stricken by no plague of locusts. Compared with the perils which our
forefathers conquered because they believed and were not afraid, we
have still much to be thankful for. Nature still offers her bounty and
human efforts have multiplied it. Plenty is at our doorstep, but a
generous use of it languishes in the very sight of the supply.

Primarily, this is because the rulers of the exchange of mankind's
goods have failed through their own stubborness and their own
incompetence, have admitted their failure and abdicated. Practices
of the unscrupulous money changers stand indicted in the court of
public opinion, rejected by the hearts and minds of men.

True, they have tried, but their efforts have been cast in the
pattern of an outworn tradition. Faced by failure of credit, they
have proposed only the lending of more money.

Stripped, of the lure of profit by which to induce our people to
follow their false leadership, they have resorted to exhortations,
pleading tearfully for restored confidence. They know only the rules
of a generation of self-seekers.

They have no vision, and when there is no vision the people
perish.

The money changers have fled from their high seats in the temple
of our civilization. We may now restore that temple to the ancient
truths.

The measure of the restoration lies in the extent to which we
apply social values more noble than mere monetary profit.

Happiness lies not in the mere possession of money; it lies in the
joy of achievement, in the thrill of creative effort.

The joy and moral stimulation of work no longer must be
forgotten in the mad chase of evanescent profits. These dark days
will be worth all they cost us if they teach us that our true destiny is
not to be ministered unto but to minister to ourselves and to our
fellow-men.

Recognition of the falsity of material wealth as the standard of
success goes hand in hand with the abandonment of the false belief
that public office and high political position are to be valued only by
the standards of pride of place and personal profit; and there must
be an end to a conduct in banking and in business which too often
has given to a sacred trust the likeness of callous and selfish
wrongdoing.

Small wonder that confidence languishes, for it thrives only on honesty, on honor, on the sacredness of obligations, on faithful protection, on unselfish performance. Without them it cannot live.

Restoration calls, however, not for changes in ethics alone. This nation asks for action, and action now.

Our greatest primary task is to put people to work. This is no unsolvable problem if we face it wisely and courageously.

It can be accomplished in part by direct recruiting by the government itself, treating the task as we would treat the emergency of a war, but at the same time, through this employment, accomplishing greatly needed projects to stimulate and reorganize the use of our natural resources.

Hand in hand with this, we must frankly recognize the overbalance of population in our industrial centers and, by engaging on a national scale in a redistribution, endeavor to provide a better use of the land for those best fitted for the land.

The task can be helped by definite efforts to raise the values of agricultural products and with this the power to purchase the output of our cities.

It can be helped by preventing realistically the tragedy of the growing loss, through foreclosure, of our small homes and our farms.

It can be helped by insistence that the Federal, State and local governments act forthwith on the demand that their cost be drastically reduced.

It can be helped by the unifying of relief activities which today are often scattered, uneconomical and unequal. It can be helped by national planning for and supervision of all forms of transportation and of communications and other utilities which have a definite public character.

There are many ways in which it can be helped, but it can never be helped merely by talking about it. We must act, and act quickly.

Finally, in our progress toward a resumption of work we require two safeguards against a return of the evils of the old order; there must be a strict supervision of all banking and credits and investments; there must be an end to speculation with other people's money, and there must be provision for an adequate but sound currency.

These are the lines of attack. I shall presently urge upon a new Congress in special session detailed measures for their fulfillment, and I shall seek the immediate assistance of the several States.

Through this program of action we address ourselves to putting our own national house in order and making income balance outgo.

Our international trade relations, though vastly important, are, in point of time and necessity, secondary to the establishment of a sound national economy.

I favor as a practical policy the putting of first things first. I shall spare no effort to restore world trade by international economic readjustment, but the emergency at home cannot wait on that accomplishment.

The basic thought that guides these specific means of national recovery is not narrowly nationalistic.

It is the insistence, as a first consideration, upon the interdependence of the various elements in, and parts of, the United States—a recognition of the old and permanently important manifestation of the American spirit of the pioneer.

It is the way to recovery. It is the immediate way. It is the strongest assurance that the recovery will endure.

In the field of world policy I would dedicate this nation to the policy of the good neighbor—the neighbor who resolutely respects himself and, because he does so, respects the rights of others—the neighbor who respects his obligations and respects the sanctity of his agreements in and with a world of neighbors.

If I read the temper of our people correctly, we now realize as we have never before, our interdependence on each other; that we cannot merely take, but we must give as well; that if we are to go forward we must move as a trained and loyal army willing to sacrifice for the good of a common discipline, because, without such discipline, no progress is made, no leadership becomes effective.

We are, I know, ready and willing to submit our lives and property to such discipline because it makes possible a leadership which aims at a larger good.

This I propose to offer, pledging that the larger purposes will bind upon us all as a sacred obligation with a unity of duty hitherto evoked only in time of armed strife.

With this pledge taken, I assume unhesitatingly the leadership of this great army of our people, dedicated to a disciplined attack upon our common problems.

Action in this image and to this end is feasible under the form of government which we have inherited from our ancestors.

Our Constitution is so simple and practical that it is possible always to meet extraordinary needs by changes in emphasis and arrangement without loss of essential form.

That is why our constitutional system has proved itself the most superbly enduring political mechanism the modern world has produced. It has met every stress of vast expansion of territory, of foreign wars, of bitter internal strife, of world relations.

It is to be hoped that the normal balance of executive and legislative authority may be wholly adequate to meet the unprecedented task before us. But it may be that an unprecedented demand and need for undelayed action may call for temporary departure from that normal balance of public procedure.

I am prepared under my constitutional duty to recommend the measures that a stricken nation in the midst of a stricken world may require.

These measures, or such other measures as the Congress may build out of its experience and wisdom, I shall seek, within my constitutional authority, to bring to speedy adoption.

But in the event that the Congress shall fail to take one of these two courses, and in the event that the national emergency is still critical, I shall not evade the clear course of duty that will then confront me.

I shall ask the Congress for the one remaining instrument to meet the crisis—broad executive power to wage a war against the emergency as great as the power that would be given me if we were in fact invaded by a foreign foe.

For the trust reposed in me I will return the courage and the devotion that befit the time. I can do no less.

We face the arduous days that lie before us in the warm courage of national unity; with the clear consciousness of seeking old and precious moral values; with the clean satisfaction that comes from the stern performance of duty by old and young alike.

We aim at the assurance of a rounded and permanent national life.

We do not distrust the future of essential democracy. The people of the United States have not failed. In their need they have registered a mandate that they want direct, vigorous action.

They have asked for discipline and direction under leadership. They have made me the present instrument of their wishes. In the spirit of the gift I take.

In this dedication of a nation we humbly ask the blessing of God. May He protect each and every one of us! May He guide me in the days to come!

5

Identification: The Audience and the Speaker

The Rhetoric of Power and Personality: Kennedy and Johnson and the Ethos of the Presidency

Attainment of the Presidency of the United States represents the ultimate achievement of a political career. The Presidency brings with it enormous power and prestige. The greatness of the office endows its holder with a significantly strong ethos and with the potential to develop his personal appeal for persuasive purposes. The presidential image, of course, is not constant. No one, including the President of the United States, can command exactly the same respect and admiration from all segments of his audience, nor is one President's ethos precisely equal to another. Some of the greatest Presidents, Abraham Lincoln and Franklin Roosevelt, for example, were cordially hated as well as revered during their administrations. But any President does command serious attention to all of his public utterances, and does gain in stature in the eyes of his audience because of the station he occupies. The two speeches that follow afford examples of the ways in which each man exploited the potential of personal appeal to promote identification with audiences.

By the third year of his presidency, John F. Kennedy had established himself as an articulate and forceful spokesman for the United States and the Western alliance. It was to shore up this alliance that Kennedy traveled to Europe in mid-1963. Although in his first year in office the young President's prestige had been shaken by the abortive "Bay of Pigs" invasion of Cuba and the unproductive and disappointing meeting with Premier Khrushchev in Vienna, by June 1963, John Kennedy had weathered the ordeal of the Cuban missile crisis of the preceding October and had demonstrated America's determination to pursue a firm policy toward the Soviet Union. This firmness was particularly welcomed in the beleaguered city of Berlin, and the citizens of West Berlin turned out to receive the President with unrestrained enthusiasm.[1] So, into the speaking situation Kennedy took a strong positive ethos.

Several tactics employed by the President supported the strategy of identification. The opening of Kennedy's speech included the traditional political custom of recognizing local leaders. The President chose to pay homage to those characteristics of the leadership of Mayor Brandt and Chancellor Adenauer that many felt Kennedy himself symbolized and that were identified in the rhetoric of the Cold War with the stalwart efforts of West Berlin to resist the pressures of Communist encirclement: He praised the Mayor's "fighting spirit" and the Chancellor's dedication to "democracy and freedom and progress." By his reference to General Clay, the American commander during the Berlin airlift, "who has been in this city during its great moments of crisis and will come again if ever needed," the President allied himself with Berlin's "savior" and underlined the determination, and the power, of the President of the United States to send help again if need be.

Playing on the abstract concepts of freedom, democracy, and progress, with which he had associated the German Chancellor and, by extension, the German people, Kennedy concretized and applied these ideals to West Berlin. The city had, as the President said, "been besieged for 18 years." The ability of the westerners to hold out and to make substantial economic gains in contrast to the starkness of the eastern half of the city, was a source of anger and outrage. Naturally enough, Kennedy recognized these feelings and identified

[1] A full account of President Kennedy's reception is found in the *New York Times*, June 27, 1963.

with them in his short address. Standing in the virtual shadow of the wall, speaking to the crowd assembled in the Rudolphe Wilde Platz, Kennedy advised those who professed not to understand "the great issue between the free world and the Communist world," those who "say that Communism is the wave of the future," those who argue that Communism "permits us to make economic progress," to do as he himself did: "Let them come to Berlin." Five times in a short paragraph the President repeated this phrase. It was a masterful and forceful emphasis of his own physical presence and a tribute to the sagacity and clear vision that results from hard experience, a vision he shared with his Berlin audience.

"On behalf of my countrymen," Kennedy expressed "the greatest pride that they have been able to share with you, even from a distance, the story of the last 18 years." And this, in a sense, is the heart of Kennedy's appeal. For he is there to share the triumph and determination of "this generation of Germans [who have] . . . earned the right to be free," and to share the agony of isolation symbolized by the wall: "an offense against humanity, separating families, dividing husbands and wives and brothers and sisters, and dividing a people who wish to be joined together."

On another level, Kennedy reminded his audience that, although they "live in a defended island of freedom," their lives are "part of the main." In a tactic that seems designed to promote the broadest possible identification, the President urged his listeners to "lift your eyes beyond the dangers of today," and stressed the essential unity of them with him, and of them and him together with all men by calling upon them to look "beyond yourselves and ourselves to all mankind." His assertion that "Freedom is indivisible, and when one man is enslaved, all are not free," is a call on the part of the President for more than unity, it is for that oneness in spirit and purpose which is an ultimate identification.

At three points in the speech, Kennedy delivered a line in German. This seems to be a decided attempt to promote identification. There was no real need to speak in German because, as the President spoke, he paused at intervals for his remarks to be translated into German. [This explains Kennedy's humorous allusion in the early part of his speech to his translator who repeated the phrase *"Ich bin ein Berliner,"* (I am a Berliner), in an obviously better German accent than Kennedy's.] Nor would the use of a few phrases do much to promote understanding. The few phrases might, however, do much to express the President's desire to compliment his audience and to strengthen his ties with them. When Kennedy first used *"Ich bin ein Berliner"* it was in comparison with the Latin *"civis Romanus sum,"* the proud boast of the ancient Roman citizen. The second use of German is the phrase *"Las' sie nach Berlin kommen"* (Let them come to Berlin), which, followed immediately by its repetition in English, culminated the passage referred to earlier, which emphasized the President's presence. But it is in his conclusion that the climax of identification was reached with the use of *"Ich bin ein Berliner"* in direct personal reference. "All free men, wherever they may live, are citizens of Berlin," the President declared, and then concluded with the words that capped his identificational strategy and drew wild cheers from his audience: "therefore, as a free man, I take pride in the words *Ich bin ein Berliner.*"

It may be said that John Kennedy's personal triumph in part is accounted for by the strong ethos that he brought with him and by his effective efforts to strengthen the bonds of identification between himself and his audience.

Scarcely five months after his successful tour of Europe, John F. Kennedy was assassinated in Dallas, and Lyndon B. Johnson succeeded to office as the thirty-sixth President of the United States. A year later Johnson was elected in his own right in an overwhelming victory over the Republican candidate, Senator Barry Goldwater of Arizona.

One of the most troubling issues with which President Johnson had to deal was civil rights. The new militancy among blacks and the fierce reaction by some whites, particularly by local governments and police in the South, had led to violent clashes. Civil rights workers were murdered in Mississippi and Alabama. Blacks and their liberal white allies were prepared to suffer indignity, outrage, and death for their cause, and some political leaders and law enforcement officers seemed equally determined to hold fast against any attempt to bring about change. The Civil Rights Act of 1964 had been emasculated, and demonstrations and protests continued after its passage. Then, in March of 1965, in Selma, Alabama, where a white clergyman was murdered and where the brutality of police and sheriff's deputies was made vividly clear to the country by television and news reports, the matter came to an ugly head. On March 15, the President of the United States appeared before a joint session of Congress to ask for specific and sweeping legislation to make up the deficiencies of the 1964 Act.

Lyndon Johnson seized the moment to use the ethos of the

Presidency to speak for the moral conscience of the nation. Before the events of the Vietnam War damaged his reputation and strained his credibility, President Johnson had not come under serious political criticism aside from that aimed at him during the campaign. There were those who, in their bitter regret over the loss of John Kennedy, could not reconcile themselves to the obvious differences in the Johnson style—whose mourning for Camelot included deprecation of the Pedernales. The avalanche of liberal hostility and denunciation was yet to come, however, and Johnson's ethos was such that he was in a position to speak for the nation.

The President, of course, was a Texan. And as a southerner he had never been an advocate of strong civil rights legislation. Indeed, his role as Senate majority leader in the passage of former civil rights legislation—legislation generally deemed ineffective by most civil rights supporters—had rendered him suspect in militant eyes. In this speech, however, Johnson used his own background and experience to bolster significantly his own image and to demonstrate his deep sincerity. In this speech, the President's brilliant use of his personal power and experience was masterful. It is his finest rhetorical effort and affords an excellent example of a speaker's promotion of identification between himself and his audience.

The President's audience, of course, was both the American public who watched the speech on their television sets and the members of both Houses of Congress. As may be seen, the President seemed not only to talk to both audiences but also to use the unseen audience at home as leverage on the immediate audience in the House chambers.

The strategy of identification followed two interwoven yet distinct lines of development, which might be described as the ethos of the public Johnson and the ethos of the private Johnson. Listeners are invited to share the power and burdens of the political leader in meeting the great moral and social challenge, and they are asked to identify with the feelings of a man of experience and deep personal conviction. As Johnson argued that "the cries of pain and the hymns and protests of oppressed people have summoned into convocation all the majesty of this great Government," he placed himself in the position of being both the head of that great Government and the spokesman in it for the oppressed people.

Speaking as the President of the United States, Johnson strove to identify his cause—"the dignity of man and the destiny of democracy"—with a great national movement of *all* Americans. The problem was "an American problem," and he was President of all

Americans. Public leader, public spokesman, and public servant are embodied in the phrase Johnson consistently employed to link the disparate elements of his audience to him; he was always "your President."

As he created the atmosphere of shared experience and sought to identify his audience with his goals and methods, President Johnson spoke of "our duty," and called upon "good men from everywhere in this country" to "rally now together." Respond, Johnson asked, to the duty "all of us owe . . . Your President makes that request of every American." And so it was as a national problem, and not just a problem for blacks, that the President viewed the situation and sought audience identification. Behind the struggle for black equality were the enemies against which the Johnson Administration, and its Democratic predecessors back to Franklin D. Roosevelt had openly and concertedly declared war: "poverty, ignorance, disease." So the aims of the civil rights movement were seen by Johnson as consistent with, even subsumed by, the aims of the Great Society upon which Johnson had so recently built a consensus.

As Johnson sought to promote identification along a broad spectrum, he did not submerge or ignore the essential question that had generated the occasion of the speech. For even as he argued that "Their cause must be our cause, too," the President was leading into an emotional moment of identification of himself with the movement. "Because it's not just Negroes but really it's all of us, who must overcome the crippling legacy of bigotry and injustice," the President said. And then he added the somewhat stunning words, "And we shall overcome." "We Shall Overcome" was the battle hymn and the battle cry of the civil rights movement. It was associated with every demonstration, every sit-in, every march, every rally. It had been sung by civil rights workers in churches, on the streets, and in jails. And now the President of the United States, in "convocation" with "the Government of the greatest nation on earth," pronounced those words from the rostrum. The President himself remembered that, just before he spoke that phrase, "A picture rose before my eyes—a picture of blacks and whites marching together, side by side, chanting and singing the anthem of the civil rights movement." [2] This was a highpoint in the speech and it was, perhaps, the climax of the civil rights movement itself. At that

[2] Lyndon Baines Johnson, *The Vantage Point, Perspective of the Presidency 1963–1969,* New York: Holt, Rinehart & Winston, 1971, p. 165.

moment all the power of government was ranged on the side of
those who, in the past, faced largely hostile agents of the community. It was an electric moment. President Johnson described it:
"For a few seconds the entire Chamber was quiet. Then the applause
started up and kept coming. One by one the Representatives and
Senators stood up. They were joined by the Cabinet, the Justices,
and the Ambassadors. Soon most of the Chamber was on its feet
with a shouting ovation that I shall never forget as long as I live." [3]
On this phrase a variety of identifications had merged.

To some, however, particularly in the South, the slogan was
anathema. Even southern moderates viewed demonstrations and
protest rallies with suspicion, and "We shall overcome" was
identified not only with civil rights but also with civil disobedience.
While he did not soften his position in the slightest regard, the
President did follow this portion of the speech immediately with the
reminder that he was "a man whose roots go deeply into Southern
soil," and that he knew "how agonizing racial feelings are." The
President who had just enunciated the rallying cry of civil rights was
also the southern man who knew "how difficult it is to reshape the
attitudes and the structure of our society." The ethos of President
Lyndon Johnson and of LBJ of Texas supplemented and comple-
mented each other.

Perhaps the most striking example of the public and private blend
that invited sympathy and understanding, was the President's story
of his teaching days in Cotulla, Texas. His moving account of the
poor and hungry students who "never seemed to know why people
disliked them" was a highly personalized one in which the frustrations of a young teacher who had seen the scars of poverty and
hatred on "the hopeful face of a young child" became strikingly
vivid. This extended example was followed by President Johnson's
rumination that he never thought that he would be able to help
these students, "But now I do have the chance." And then, in a
sharp and forceful aside, which reminded the audience that the
young teacher was now the President of the United States—and a
President who was fully aware of his power and determined to
exercise it—Johnson added, "And I'll let you in on a secret—I mean
to use it." All those who had been frustrated themselves by injustice,
or who had despaired of ever seeing wrongs righted, could identify

[3] *Ibid.*, pp. 165–166.

with the power of this very real man who now wielded the authority
to bring about change.

A further example of the blending of Johnson's public and private
ethos is afforded by the President's references to Congress. On the
one hand, he reminded the assembled senators and representatives
that they, with him, had "sworn an oath before God to support and
defend that Constitution," and urged that "We must now act in
obedience to that oath"; on the other hand, he spoke of the
opportunity to "reason with my friends, to give them my views and
to visit with my former colleagues." Johnson had, indeed, worked
closely with his fellow members of Congress for many years and he
could both reinforce this old tie, make humorous references to the
"suggestions from all members of Congress," and call for close
harmony between the two branches of government. In the closing
minutes of the speech the President, who had earlier asked Congress
to join him "in working long hours and nights and weekends, if
necessary, to pass this bill," now reminded them that he had not
come from the White House to confront the Congress; on the
contrary: "I came down here to ask you to share this task with me.
And to share it with the people that we both work for."

Using the authority and prestige of the Presidency, coupled with
his personal, compassionate experience, Lyndon Johnson sought to
strengthen the bonds of identification between himself and his
audience. This speech must stand as a fine example of such an effort.

JOHN F. KENNEDY

ICH BIN EIN BERLINER

I am proud to come to this city as the guest of your distinguished Mayor, who has symbolized throughout the world the

John F. Kennedy's speech was given in Berlin on June 26, 1963. It is
reprinted from *Public Papers of the Presidents of the United States: John F.
Kennedy: Containing the Public Messages, Speeches, and Statements of the
President: January 1 to November 22, 1963*, Washington, D.C.: GPO, 1964,
item 269, pp. 525–552.

fighting spirit of West Berlin. And I am proud to visit the Federal Republic with your distinguished Chancellor who for so many years has committed Germany to democracy and freedom and progress, and to come here in the company of my fellow American, General Clay, who has been in this city during its great moments of crisis and will come again if ever needed.

Two thousand years ago the proudest boast was *"civis Romanus sum."* Today, in the world of freedom, the proudest boast is *"Ich bin ein Berliner."*

I appreciate my interpreter translating my German!

There are many people in the world who really don't understand, or say they don't, what is the great issue between the free world and the Communist world. Let them come to Berlin. There are some who say that communism is the wave of the future. Let them come to Berlin. And there are some who say in Europe and elsewhere we can work with the Communists. Let them come to Berlin. And there are even a few who say that it is true that communism is an evil system, but it permits us to make economic progress. *Lass' sie nach Berlin kommen.* Let them come to Berlin.

Freedom has many difficulties and democracy is not perfect, but we have never had to put a wall up to keep our people in, to prevent them from leaving us. I want to say, on behalf of my countrymen, who live many miles away on the other side of the Atlantic, who are far distant from you, that they take the greatest pride that they have been able to share with you, even from a distance, the story of the last 18 years. I know of no town, no city, that has been besieged for 18 years that still lives with the vitality and the force, and the hope and the determination of the city of West Berlin. While the wall is the most obvious and vivid demonstration of the failures of the Communist system, for all the world to see, we take no satisfaction in it, for it is, as your Mayor has said, an offense not only against history but an offense against humanity, separating families, dividing husbands and wives and brothers and sisters, and dividing a people who wish to be joined together.

What is true of this city is true of Germany—real, lasting peace in Europe can never be assured as long as one German out of four is denied the elementary right of free men, and that is to make a free choice. In 18 years of peace and good faith, this generation of Germans has earned the right to be free, including the right to unite their families and their nation in lasting peace, with good will to all people. You live in a defended island of freedom, but your life is

part of the main. So let me ask you, as I close, to lift your eyes
beyond the dangers of today, to the hopes of tomorrow, beyond the
freedom merely of this city of Berlin, or your country of Germany,
to the advance of freedom everywhere, beyond the wall to the day
of peace with justice, beyond yourselves and ourselves to all
mankind.

Freedom is indivisible, and when one man is enslaved, all are not
free. When all are free, then we can look forward to that day when
this city will be joined as one and this country and this great
Continent of Europe in a peaceful and hopeful globe. When that day
finally comes, as it will, the people of West Berlin can take sober
satisfaction in the fact that they were in the front lines for almost
two decades.

All free men, wherever they may live, are citizens of Berlin, and
therefore, as a free man, I take pride in the words *Ich bin ein
Berliner.*

LYNDON B. JOHNSON

WE SHALL OVERCOME

Mr. Speaker, Mr. President, members of the Congress, I speak
tonight for the dignity of man and the destiny of democracy. I urge
every member of both parties, Americans of all religions and of all
colors, from every section of this country, to join me in that cause.

At times, history and fate meet at a single time in a single place to
shape a turning point in man's unending search for freedom.

So it was at Lexington and Concord. So it was a century ago at
Appomattox. So it was last week in Selma, Alabama.

There, long suffering men and women peacefully protested the
denial of their rights as Americans. Many of them were brutally
assaulted. One good man—a man of God—was killed.

There is no cause for pride in what has happened in Selma. There
is no cause for self-satisfaction in the long denial of equal rights of

Lyndon B. Johnson's speech was given in Washington, D.C., on March 15,
1964. It is reprinted from the *Congressional Record, House of Representatives,* March 15, 1964, pp. 5059–5061.

millions of Americans. But there is cause for hope and for faith in our democracy in what is happening here tonight.

For the cries of pain and the hymns and protests of oppressed people have summoned into convocation all the majesty of this great Government—the Government of the greatest nation on earth.

Our mission is at once the oldest and the most basic of this country—to right wrong, to do justice, to serve man.

In our time we have come to live with the moments of great crisis. Our lives have been marked with debate about great issues, issues of war and peace, issues of prosperity and depression.

But rarely in any time does an issue lay bare the secret heart of America itself. Rarely are we met with a challenge, not to our growth or abundance, or our welfare or our security, but rather to the values and the purposes and the meaning of our beloved nation.

The issue of equal rights for American Negroes is such an issue.

And should we defeat every enemy, and should we double our wealth and conquer the stars, and still be unequal to this issue, then we will have failed as a people and as a nation.

For, with a country as with a person, "What is a man profited if he shall gain the whole world, and lose his own soul?"

There is no Negro problem. There is no Southern problem. There is no Northern problem. There is only an American problem.

And we are met here tonight as Americans—not as Democrats or Republicans; we're met here as Americans to solve that problem.

This was the first nation in the history of the world to be founded with a purpose. The great phrases of that purpose still sound in every American heart, North and South:

"All men are created equal." "Government by consent of the governed." "Give me liberty or give me death."

And those are not just clever words, and those are not just empty theories.

In their name Americans have fought and died for two centuries and tonight around the world they stand there as guardians of our liberty risking their lives.

Those words are promised to every citizen that he shall share in the dignity of man. This dignity cannot be found in a man's possessions. It cannot be found in his power or in his position. It really rests on his right to be treated as a man equal in opportunity to all others.

It says that he shall share in freedom. He shall choose his leaders, educate his children, provide for his family according to his ability and his merits as a human being.

To apply any other test, to deny a man his hopes because of his color or race or his religion or the place of his birth is not only to do injustice, it is to deny Americans and to dishonor the dead who gave their lives for American freedom.

Our fathers believed that if this noble view of the rights of man was to flourish it must be rooted in democracy. The most basic right of all was the right to choose your own leaders.

The history of this country in large measure is the history of expansion of that right to all of our people. Many of the issues of civil rights are very complex and most difficult. But about this there can and should be no argument: every American citizen must have an equal right to vote.

There is no reason which can excuse the denial of that right. There is no duty which weighs more heavily on us than the duty we have to insure that right. Yet the harsh fact is that in many places in this country men and women are kept from voting simply because they are Negroes.

Every device of which human ingenuity is capable has been used to deny this right. The Negro citizen may go to register only to be told that the day is wrong, or the hour is late, or the official in charge is absent.

And if he persists and, if he manages to present himself to the registrar, he may be disqualified because he did not spell out his middle name, or because he abbreviated a word on the application. And if he manages to fill out an application, he is given a test.

The registrar is the sole judge of whether he passes this test. He may be asked to recite the entire Constitution or explain the most complex provisions of state law.

And even a college degree cannot be used to prove that he can read and write. For the fact is that the only way to pass these barriers is to show a white skin.

Experience has clearly shown that the existing process of law cannot overcome systematic and ingenious discrimination. No law that we now have on the books, and I have helped to put three of them there, can insure the right to vote when local officials are determined to deny it. In such a case, our duty must be clear to all of us.

The Constitution says that no person shall be kept from voting because of his race or his color. We have all sworn an oath before God to support and to defend that Constitution. We must now act in obedience to that oath.

Wednesday, I will send to Congress a law designed to eliminate illegal barriers to the right to vote.

The broad principles of that bill will be in the hands of the Democratic and Republican leaders tomorrow. After they have reviewed it, it will come here formally as a bill.

I am grateful for this opportunity to come here tonight at the invitation of the leadership to reason with my friends, to give them my views and to visit with my former colleagues.

I have had prepared a more comprehensive analysis of the legislation which I had intended to transmit to the clerk tomorrow, but which I will submit to the clerks tonight. But I want to really discuss the main proposals of this legislation.

This bill will strike down restrictions to voting in all elections, Federal, state and local, which have been used to deny Negroes the right to vote.

This bill will establish a simple, uniform standard which cannot be used, however ingenious the effort, to flout our Constitution. It will provide for citizens to be registered by officials of the United States Government, if the state officials refuse to register them.

It will eliminate tedious, unnecessary lawsuits which delay the right to vote.

Finally, this legislation will insure that properly registered individuals are not prohibited from voting.

I will welcome the suggestions from all the members of Congress— I have no doubt that I will get some—on ways and means to strengthen this law and to make it effective.

But experience has plainly shown that this is the only path to carry out the command of the Constitution. To those who seek to avoid action by their national Government in their home communities, who want to and who seek to maintain purely local control over elections, the answer is simple: Open your polling places to all your people.

Allow men and women to register and vote whatever the color of their skin.

Extend the rights of citizenship to every citizen of this land.

There is no constitutional issue here. The command of the Constitution is plain. There is no moral issue. It is wrong—deadly wrong—to deny any of your fellow Americans the right to vote in this country.

There is no issue of state's rights or national rights. There is only the struggle for human rights.

I have not the slightest doubt what will be your answer. But the last time a President sent a civil rights bill to the Congress it contained a provision to protect voting rights in Federal elections. That civil rights bill was passed after eight long months of debate. And when that bill came to my desk from the Congress for signature, the heart of the voting provision had been eliminated.

This time, on this issue, there must be no delay, or no hesitation, or no compromise with our purpose.

We cannot, we must not, refuse to protect the right of every American to vote in every election that he may desire to participate in.

And we ought not, and we cannot, and we must not wait another eight months before we get a bill.

We have already waited 100 years and more and the time for waiting is gone.

So I ask you to join me in working long hours and nights and weekends, if necessary, to pass this bill.

And I don't make that request lightly, for from the window where I sit with the problems of our country I recognize that from outside this chamber is the outraged conscience of a nation, the grave concern of many nations and the harsh judgment of history on our acts.

But even if we pass this bill the battle will not be over.

What happened in Selma is part of a far larger movement which reaches into every section and state of America. It is the effort of American Negroes to secure for themselves the full blessings of American life.

Their cause must be our cause too. Because it's not just Negroes but really it's all of us, who must overcome the crippling legacy of bigotry and injustice.

And we shall overcome.

As a man whose roots go deeply into Southern soil, I know how agonizing racial feelings are. I know how difficult it is to reshape the attitudes and the structure of our society. But a century has passed—more than 100 years—since the Negro was freed.

And he is not fully free tonight.

It was more than 100 years ago that Abraham Lincoln—a great President of another party—signed the Emancipation Proclamation. But emancipation is a proclamation and not a fact.

A century has passed—more than 100 years—since equality was promised, and yet the Negro is not equal.

A century has passed since the day of promise, and the promise is unkept. The time of justice has now come, and I tell you that I believe sincerely that no force can hold it back. It is right in the eyes of man and God that it should come, and when it does, I think that day will brighten the lives of every American.

For Negroes are not the only victims. How many white children have gone uneducated? How many white families have lived in stark poverty? How many white lives have been scarred by fear, because we wasted energy and our substance to maintain the barriers of hatred and terror?

And so I say to all of you here and to all in the nation tonight that those who appeal to you to hold on to the past do so at the cost of denying you your future. This great rich, restless country can offer opportunity and education and hope to all—all, black and white, North and South, sharecropper and city dweller.

These are the enemies: poverty, ignorance, disease. They are our enemies, not our fellow man, not our neighbor. And these enemies too—poverty, disease and ignorance—we shall overcome.

Now let none of us in any section look with prideful righteousness on the troubles in another section or the problems of our neighbors.

There is really no part of America where the promise of equality has been fully kept. In Buffalo as well as in Birmingham, in Philadelphia as well as Selma, Americans are struggling for the fruits of freedom. This is one nation. What happens in Selma and Cincinnati is a matter of legitimate concern to every American.

But let each of us look within our own hearts and our own communities and let each of us put our shoulder to the wheel to root out injustice wherever it exists.

As we meet here in this peaceful historic chamber tonight, men from the South, some of whom were at Iwo Jima, men from the North who have carried Old Glory to the far corners of the world and who brought it back without a stain on it, men from the East and from the West are all fighting together without regard to religion or color or region in Vietnam. Men from every region fought for us across the world 20 years ago. And now in these common dangers, in these common sacrifices, the South made its contribution of honor and gallantry no less than any other region in the Great Republic. And in some instances, a great many of them, more.

And I have not the slightest doubt that good men from everywhere in this country, from the Great Lakes to the Gulf of Mexico, from the Golden Gate to the harbors along the Atlantic, will rally now together in this cause to vindicate the freedom of all Americans.

For all of us owe this duty and I believe that all of us will respond to it. Your President makes that request of every American.

The real hero of this struggle is the American Negro. His actions and protests, his courage to risk safety, and even to risk his life, have awakened the conscience of this nation. His demonstrations have been designed to call attention to injustice, designed to provoke change; designed to stir reform.

He has been called upon to make good the promise of America. And who among us can say that we would have made the same progress were it not for his persistent bravery and his faith in American democracy?

For at the real heart of the battle for equality is a deep-seated belief in the democratic process. Equality depends, not on the force of arms or tear gas, but depends upon the force of moral right—not on recourse to violence, but on respect for law and order.

There have been many pressures upon your President and there will be others as the days come and go. But I pledge to you tonight that we intend to fight this battle where it should be fought—in the courts, and in the Congress, and in the hearts of men.

We must preserve the right of free speech and the right of free assembly.

But the right of free speech does not carry with it—as has been said—the right to holler fire in a crowded theater.

We must preserve the right to free assembly. But free assembly does not carry with it the right to block public thoroughfares to traffic.

We do have a right to protest. And a right to march under conditions that do not infringe the constitutional rights of our neighbors. And I intend to protect all those rights as long as I am permitted to serve in this office.

We will guard against violence, knowing it strikes from our hands the very weapons which we seek—progress, obedience to law, and belief in American values.

In Selma, as elsewhere, we seek and pray for peace. We seek order, we seek unity, but we will not accept the peace of stifled rights or the order imposed by fear, or the unity that stifles protest—for peace cannot be purchased at the cost of liberty.

In Selma tonight—and we had a good day there—as in every city we are working for a just and peaceful settlement. We must all remember after this speech I'm making tonight, after the police and the F.B.I. and the marshals have all gone, and after you have promptly passed this bill, the people of Selma and the other cities of the nation must still live and work together.

And when the attention of the nation has gone elsewhere they must try to heal the wounds and to build a new community. This cannot be easily done on a battle ground of violence as the history of the South itself shows. It is in recognition of this that men of both races have shown such an outstandingly impressive responsibility in recent days—last Tuesday and again today.

The bill I am presenting to you will be known as a civil rights bill.

But in a larger sense, most of the program I am recommending is a civil rights program. Its object is to open the city of hope to all people of all races, because all Americans just must have the right to vote, and we are going to give them that right.

All Americans must have the privileges of citizenship, regardless of race, and they are going to have those privileges of citizenship regardless of race.

But I would like to caution you and remind you that to exercise these privileges takes much more than just legal right. It requires a trained mind and a healthy body. It requires a decent home and the chance to find a job and the opportunity to escape from the clutches of poverty.

Of course people cannot contribute to the nation if they are never taught to read or write; if their bodies are stunted from hunger; if their sickness goes untended; if their life is spent in hopeless poverty, just drawing a welfare check.

So we want to open the gates to opportunity. But we're also going to give all our people, black and white, the help that they need to walk through those gates.

My first job after college was as a teacher in Cotulla, Texas, in a small Mexican-American school. Few of them could speak English and I couldn't speak much Spanish.

My students were poor and they often came to class without breakfast and hungry. And they knew even in their youth the pain of prejudice. They never seemed to know why people disliked them, but they knew it was so because I saw it in their eyes.

I often walked home late in the afternoon after the classes were finished wishing there was more that I could do. But all I knew was to teach them the little that I knew, hoping that it might help them against the hardships that lay ahead.

And somehow you never forget what poverty and hatred can do when you see its scars on the hopeful face of a young child.

I never thought then, in 1928, that I would be standing here in 1965. It never even occurred to me in my fondest dreams that I might have the chance to help the sons and daughters of those students, and to help people like them all over this country.

But now I do have that chance. And I'll let you in on a secret—I mean to use it.

And I hope that you will use it with me. This is the richest, most powerful country which ever occupied this globe. The might of past empires is little compared to ours. But I do not want to be the President who built empires, or sought grandeur, or extended dominion. I want to be the President who educated young children to the wonders of their world.

I want to be the President who helped to feed the hungry and to prepare them to be taxpayers instead of tax eaters.

I want to be the President who helped the poor to find their own way and who protected the right of every citizen to vote in every election.

I want to be the President who helped to end hatred among his fellow men and who promoted love among the people of all races, all regions and all parties.

I want to be the President who helped to end war among the brothers of this earth.

And so at the request of your beloved Speaker and the Senator from Montana, the majority leader, the Senator from Illinois, the minority leader, Mr. McCulloch and other members of both parties, I came here tonight, not as President Roosevelt came down one time in person to veto a bonus bill; not as President Truman came down one time to urge the passage of a railroad bill, but I came down here to ask you to share this task with me. And to share it with the people that we both work for.

I want this to be the Congress—Republicans and Democrats alike—which did all these things for all these people.

Beyond this great chamber—out yonder—in fifty states are the people that we serve. Who can tell what deep and unspoken hopes are in their hearts tonight as they sit there and listen?

We all can guess, from our own lives, how difficult they often find their own pursuit of happiness.

How many problems each little family has. They look most of all to themselves for their future, but I think they also look to each of us.

Above the pyramid on the great seal of the United States it says in Latin, "God has favored our undertaking." God will not favor everything we do. It is rather our duty to divine His will. But I cannot help but believe that He truly understands and that He really favors the undertaking that we begin here tonight.

6

The Quality
of Reasonableness

Reason in Compromise and Crisis:
Franklin and Wilkins on the
Republican Experiment

As he ended his speech to the NAACP in 1966, Roy Wilkins warned that "The republican experiment is at stake." Indeed, throughout American history the basic principle of democratic self-government has been threatened and challenged, and the extent to which this principle is being and can be implemented to bring about full equality and justice is a matter of widespread and serious current concern. The following speeches are the attempts of two different kinds of leaders to reason with their associates at two critical points in the life of the "experiment": Benjamin Franklin's speech delivered to the Constitutional Convention in 1787 at the inception of the republic, and Roy Wilkins' speech given to the NAACP in 1966, when racial unrest and turmoil characterized the growing black revolution.

Benjamin Franklin was past eighty and too frail to deliver his own speech at the closing of the Constitutional Convention.[1] The venerable Dr. Franklin, long active in colonial political affairs, present at sessions of the Continental Congress that produced the Declaration of Independence, a principal author of the Pennsylvania

[1] The speech was read to the Convention by a colleague from Pennsylvania, James Wilson.

Constitution, our first ambassador to France, had earned the title of elder statesman. A celebrated philosopher and scientist as well as a political figure, he was held in high esteem by the delegates assembled in Philadelphia. Franklin did not take an active part in the debates themselves, but once the compromises had finally been reached and the document framed he sought to infuse the delegates with a spirit of unity and purpose necessary to secure its adoption by the state legislatures.

In his very short speech, Franklin attempted to convince the delegates that they should sign the document before them and, more than that, that they should join together to present a united front to those at home and abroad waiting to hear the results of their deliberations. In order to do this, Franklin developed two principal arguments: First, the resulting Constitution was the best code that could have been devised given the normal failings of the human situation; and, second, any personal reservations that delegates might have should be submerged for the sake of "real or apparent unanimity."

Franklin spent a relatively large portion of his speech discussing human fallibility in support of the first argument directly, and of the second indirectly. The long, hard Convention debates had been marked by compromise. Widely different views had been strongly held and fiercely advocated, yet accommodation of conflicting proposals had finally been reached. The result was not likely to be what any single delegate would most have wanted nor did it approximate any single participant's ideal constitution. Franklin's initial statement, "I confess I do not entirely approve of this Constitution at present," must have been a sentiment shared by his audience. Now certainly the generalization that no man is infallible does not seem to be an argument that needs much support. While this proposition may be accepted in the abstract, however, Franklin was wise enough to know that it was more difficult for a man to apply it directly to himself in a specific situation. Even though it was an assumption that his audience might be expected to accept, it was eminently reasonable of Franklin to devote some attention to elaborating on it.

Franklin chose to develop the argument by first exploiting his own ethos. "I have experienced many instances," Franklin averred, "of being obliged, by better information or fuller consideration, to change opinions even on important subjects, which I once thought right, but found to be otherwise." And it is this personal experience that lead him to observe that "the older I grow, the more apt I am to doubt my own judgment of others." As further evidence, Franklin produced additional support, which, couched as it is in the typical Franklin wit, tended to suggest the slightly ridiculous aspect of failure to admit error: the quotation from Steele comparing the Roman Church, which is "infallible," and the Church of England, which is "never in the wrong," and the anecdote concerning the French lady who is "always in the right."

With this evidence before the delegates, Franklin was able to go on to lay out his first major contention: "I doubt, too, whether any other convention we can obtain, may be able to make a better Constitution." This generalization came from the general observations regarding human fallibility; he supported it further with a specific reference to a condition that men in political life could hardly have failed to experience: "when you assemble a number of men to have the advantage of their joint wisdom, you inevitably assemble with those men, all their prejudices, their passions, their errors of opinion, their local interests, and their selfish views." The answer to the rhetorical question that follows—"From such an assembly can a *perfect* production be expected?"—is obvious, and Franklin had prepared carefully for this question.

As the speech continued, Franklin merged this first argument with his second, tying the two together, demonstrating how one grows out of the other, in an excellent transitional section, before proceeding to develop the second argument. For as Franklin professed his astonishment at how fine a document had, indeed, been produced despite human failings, he foreshadowed his next argument by adding, "and I think it will astonish our enemies, who are waiting with confidence to hear that our counsels are confounded like those of the builders of Babel, and that our States are on the point of separation, only to meet hereafter for the purpose of cutting one another's throats." Still in transition, Franklin followed immediately with a final statement of his first argument and opened his second: "Thus I consent, sir, to this Constitution, because I expect no better, and because I am not sure that it is not the best. The opinions I have had of its *errors* I sacrifice to the public good."

The second argument, the call for unity, was offered in the context of the rules under which the debate had proceeded. A strict secrecy had been maintained; delegates had spoken freely and candidly without fear of public reaction to their statements, and outside of the Convention little was known of what had transpired.

The compromises reached had been hard won. Franklin obviously feared that some might wish to reargue their cases in the ratifying conventions, thus contributing to the destruction of the carefully built compromises and affording opponents the opportunity to argue that even those who had framed the Constitution were dissatisfied with it. Such a spectacle, Franklin argued in support of his contention, would imperil "the salutary effects and great advantages resulting naturally in our favor among foreign nations, as well as among ourselves, from our real or apparent unanimity." In essence, Franklin's support for his second argument was an elaboration of the rhetorically strategic advantage of presenting a discrete entity, the Constitution as a whole, firmly grounded in the collective advocacy of the political leaders who had composed it. Not only would foreign governments be impressed, and Franklin had alluded to foreign enemies previously, but the domestic "general opinion" would be convinced of "the goodness of that government, as well as of the wisdom and integrity of its governors." Franklin knew, however, that there were those in his audience whose reservations were serious. To those who harbored doubts of the adequacy of the Constitution, Franklin offered an alternative to opposition to its adoption. Those members he urged to direct their attention to administration of the Constitution after its adoption. Early in the speech he had enunciated the principle "there is no *form* of government but what may be a blessing to the people, if well administered," and in closing he urged his listeners to "act heartily and unanimously in recommending this Constitution, wherever our influence may extend, and turn our future thoughts and endeavors to the means of having it *well administered*."

There appeared in Franklin's speech one assertion that is virtually unsupported and yet most basic to Franklin's message and, indeed, to the entire process of framing and adopting the Constitution. As Franklin announced that he agreed "to this Constitution with all its faults," he went on to explain, "because I think a general government necessary for us." There has been much debate among historians about the reasons for the calling of the Constitutional Convention.[2] It is hardly controversial, however, to assert that most

[2] For an introduction to the debate among historians see Earl Lantham, ed., *The Declaration of Independence and the Constitution*, rev. ed., Boston: Heath, 1956. I have discussed this matter from a rhetorical point of view in "The Rhetoric of History: The Constitutional Convention," *Today's Speech: The Journal of the Speech Association of the Eastern States*, 16:4 (November 1968), 23–26.

members of the Convention itself felt a need for government reform and constitutional change. This assertion by Franklin is based on the clearly held assumption of the audience that a "general government" of some kind was necessary. Franklin's behavior in this regard affords an excellent example of the relativity of reason, for certainly the audience could be expected to accept such a statement without proof or elaboration; it appeared perfectly "reasonable" to most of them, and to develop it at this point in the proceedings would have been unnecessary and tedious.

This short speech, then, shows the enunciation and development of, and relationships between, arguments that are perfectly "reasonable." They are so because the nature of the audience, the ethos of the speaker, and the occasion itself are in harmony with the generalizations, evidence, and assumptions on which the speech is built.

Nearly two hundred years later, Roy Wilkins, Executive Secretary of the NAACP, faced the delegates to that organization's convention at a time when the struggle for black equality held the attention of the nation. In 1965, the Watts riots in Los Angeles stunned the country, and in June 1966, shortly before Wilkins spoke, James Meredith was shot from ambush as he marched through Mississippi. Floyd McKissick of CORE, Stokely Carmichael of SNCC, and Martin Luther King, as well as leaders of the NAACP, had joined to carry on the Meredith march. Although achieving some semblance of unity, black spokesmen could not uniformly agree on the meaning of the slogan "black power," or on the implications it held for the strategy and goals of the civil rights movement.[3]

Young, militant blacks had obviously become dissatisfied with the slow progress of the civil rights movement and were challenging the efficacy of the old methods in producing serious change as well as the basic assumption that racial integration was, itself, the ultimate goal. Wilkins reacted strongly to this challenge.

The NAACP with its tradition of legal activism, its large middle-class black membership, its significant white support, was generally considered a more conservative civil rights organization. Wilkins' audience of moderate blacks and their white allies heard the speech in the context of the confusion and disquiet that the black power

---

[3] See Robert L. Scott and Wayne Brockriede, *The Rhetoric of Black Power*, New York: Harper & Row, 1969. A short account of the civil rights movement is also found in the introduction to Haig A. Bosmajian and Homida Bosmajian, *The Rhetoric of the Civil Rights Movement*, New York: Random House, 1969.

slogan had produced. Furthermore, Wilkins faced a problem that Franklin, speaking only to an immediate audience did not encounter. In addition to those gathered at the convention, Wilkins' words would be widely reported to an outside audience of blacks and whites of various sympathies and persuasions. A statement by a major black leader on the burning issue of black power would be eminently newsworthy.

Wilkins' argumentative strategy is based on two principal contentions: first, that the methods and goals suggested by "black power" advocates are basically unproductive and, further, are antithetical to the achievement of black equality in the context of human brotherhood; and, second, that the methods of the NAACP have produced gains for blacks and should continue to merit both black and white support as the struggle went on. Offensive and defensive elements are mixed in these two arguments but, basically the first argument is offensive and the second defensive.

The chain of reasoning that leads to the denunciation of black power began with a juxtaposition of violence and nonviolence. "There has now emerged," Wilkins asserted, "a strident and threatening challenge to a strategy widely employed by civil rights groups, namely nonviolence." Citing an example to support this dichotomy, Wilkins pointed to the action of CORE, which had "passed a resolution declaring for defense of themselves by Negro citizens if they are attacked." Wilkins' development of this point is interesting. For rather than bringing to bear additional evidence to show the violent nature of black power, he detailed historical examples to show that the NAACP had given legal support to those blacks who had acted in self-defense, and maintained, "but we have never required this [nonviolence] as a deep personal commitment of our members. We never signed a pact either on paper or in our hearts to turn the other cheek forever and ever when we were assaulted." He does not, then, take issue with the basic right of the black man to defend himself, but, rather, finds the *statement* of such a right inflammatory, suggesting that it compels blacks "to maintain themselves in an armed state, ready to attack instantly and in kind whenever attacked." This distinction, taken together with the warning that follows, lays bare a crucial assumption in Wilkins' reasoning. For his fear of "counter-action," of "indiscriminate crackdown by law officers," reveals the assumption that the black power call is one to aggressive violence, not really self-defense, and is a prelude to violent revolution. Only such an assumption makes Wilkins' defense of the NAACP's actions in 1919 and 1926 in providing legal help for those who had fought back against violent assault essentially different from the CORE resolution and, hence, understandable. The acceptance of this particular distinction in method as the critical one between black power advocates, and Wilkins depends, accordingly, on the acceptance of that assumption. For such acceptance, however, the listener would have to go beyond the speech itself, which does not present evidence pertinent to this point.

As he moved to a discussion of the goals of black power, Wilkins clearly stated the assumption upon which this phase of the argument was based: "No matter how endlessly they try to explain it, the term 'black power' means anti-white." The phrase "No matter how endlessly they try to explain it" is a dismissal of all counterinterpretations of black power by its supporters. Wilkins eschews all concrete evidence to support his interpretation; not once does he refer to the words or actions of black power leaders. It may be that Wilkins felt that this was obvious to those auditors at whom he aimed his speech—middle-class, conservative blacks, and whites who were, by and large, suspicious and frightened by black power—or that his own strong emotional reaction caused him to dismiss other views as those of a militant fringe. In any case, this basic contention concerning the goals of black power is followed only by a long series of unsupported assertions, which lead him to castigate "separatism," claim that the black power ideology "dictates 'up with black and down with white,' " and describe the movement as "a reverse Mississippi, a reverse Hitler, a reverse Ku Klux Klan." "We of the NAACP will have none of this," said Wilkins closing the argument. "We have fought it too long." And he finally characterized black power as "the ranging of race against race on the irrelevant basis of skin color. It is the father of hatred and mother of violence."

With the passage of time, the black power spectre has lost most of its frightfulness, and Wilkins should certainly not be blamed for being unable to predict the future. But certainly his argument did little to make distinctions clearer on the basis of reasoned analysis, nor does it show a determination to examine assumptions in the cold, dispassionate light of hard evidence.

On the second argument, that of the accomplishments of the NAACP and its understanding of the areas of black concern, Wilkins brought more evidence to bear upon his generalizations. Here he was specific as he outlined five choices that the NAACP would make in its "Fight for Freedom."

The first was primarily strategic and was obviously meant to stand in contrast to his conception of black power: "[We choose] The power and majesty of the ballot, the participation of free men in their government, both as voters and as honorable and competent elected and appointed public officials." Wilkins' assertion is that the democratic system can be made to work by and for the black man. He cited voter registration figures in Mississippi, pointed to plans for a registration drive in Louisiana, and indicated the appointment of a southern black to the board of governors of the Federal Reserve Bank. And throughout his discussion of other "choices," Wilkins refers to specific and general lobbying and legal activities of the organization that bear testimony to his own conviction that exploiting the full potentials of the present system must be the choice of the civil rights movement.

As he described the problems of employment, housing, education, and urban life, Wilkins sought, by specific example as well as by specific criticism of public officials and acts he considered hostile to civil rights, to show that the NAACP achieved success in the past and was moving in the right direction for the future. The reasoning is clear and the evidence, while not extensive, is pertinent to Wilkins' argument.

But no doubt Wilkins and his audience were aware of the criticism that traditional civil rights groups had achieved relatively little, that at best "tokenism" had resulted from tremendous and agonizing effort, that "Uncle Tomism" had infected the old-fashioned leadership. Woven within the pattern of argument is Wilkins' refusal to accept this indictment. His review of the racial problems facing America, and his recognition that many very serious problems still exist, ended with the admonition to his audience: "But in this unsettled time when shifts are the order of the day and when change is in the air, we shall sail our NAACP ship 'steady as she goes,' with more drive to the turbines, more skill at the wheel, but no fancy capers for the sake of capers." "Steady as she goes," clearly implies more of the same; Wilkins ended his speech with a long enumeration of specific programs and a call to continue exerting pressure through "every legitimate technique: protests, surveys, discussions, demonstrations, picketing and negotiation."

The rhetorical circumstances under which the Wilkins' speech was given—a time of great controversy and division within the civil rights movement itself—suggest that Wilkins' attack on black power was not a reasonable one, but his attempt to speak for the NAACP and its achievements and potential contained a more careful weighing of evidence and a more rational effort to relate evidence to generalizations and conclusions.

BENJAMIN FRANKLIN

ON THE CONSTITUTION

Mr. President:—I confess that I do not entirely approve of this Constitution at present; but, sir, I am not sure I shall never approve it; for, having lived long, I have experienced many instances of being obliged, by better information or fuller consideration, to change opinions even on important subjects, which I once thought right, but found to be otherwise. It is therefore that, the older I grow, the more apt I am to doubt my own judgment of others. Most men, indeed, as well as most sects in religion, think themselves in possession of all truth, and that wherever others differ from them, it is so far error. Steele, a Protestant, in a dedication, tells the Pope that the only difference between our two churches in their opinions of the certainty of their doctrine is, the Romish Church is infallible, and the Church of England is never in the wrong. But though many private persons think almost as highly of their own infallibility as that of their sect, few express it so naturally as a certain French lady, who, in a little dispute with her sister, said: "But I meet with nobody but myself that is always in the right." *"Je ne troube que moi qui aie toujours raison."*

In these sentiments, sir, I agree to this Constitution, with all its faults—if they are such;—because I think a general government necessary for us, and there is no form of government but what may be a blessing to the people, if well administered; and I believe further, that this is likely to be well administered for a course of years, and can only end in despotism, as other forms have done before it, when the people shall become so corrupted as to need

Benjamin Franklin's speech was given in Philadelphia on September 17, 1787. It is reprinted from John Bigelow, ed., *The Complete Works of Benjamin Franklin*, New York: Putnam, 1888, vol. IX, pp. 431–433.

despotic government, being incapable of any other. I doubt, too, whether any other convention we can obtain, may be able to make a better Constitution; for when you assemble a number of men, to have the advantage of their joint wisdom, you inevitably assemble with those men, all their prejudices, their passions, their errors of opinion, their local interests, and their selfish views. From such an assembly can a perfect production be expected? It therefore astonishes me, sir, to find this system approaching so near to perfection as it does; and I think it will astonish our enemies, who are waiting with confidence to hear that our counsels are confounded like those of the builders of Babel, and that our States are on the point of separation, only to meet hereafter for the purpose of cutting one another's throats. Thus I consent, sir, to this Constitution, because I expect no better, and because I am not sure that it is not the best. The opinions I have had of its errors I sacrifice to the public good. I have never whispered a syllable of them abroad. Within these walls they were born, and here they shall die. If every one of us, in returning to our constituents, were to report the objections he has had to it, and endeavor to gain partisans in support of them, we might prevent its being generally received, and thereby lose all the salutary effects and great advantages resulting naturally in our favor among foreign nations, as well as among ourselves, from our real or apparent unanimity. Much of the strength and efficiency of any government in procuring and securing happiness to the people, depends on opinion, on the general opinion, of the goodness of that government, as well as of the wisdom and integrity of its governors. I hope, therefore, for our own sakes, as a part of the people, and for the sake of our posterity, that we shall act heartily and unanimously in recommending this Constitution, wherever our influence may extend, and turn our future thoughts and endeavors to the means of having it well administered.

On the whole, sir, I cannot help expressing a wish that every member of the convention who may still have objections to it would with me on this occasion doubt a little of his own infallibility, and, to make manifest our unanimity, put his name to this instrument.

ROY WILKINS

KEYNOTE ADDRESS TO THE NAACP
ANNUAL CONVENTION

In the transition period of the civil rights movement, 1966 is
developing into a critical year. The 57th annual convention of our
NAACP is thus a gathering of more than ordinary significance.

All about us are alarms and confusions as well as great and
challenging developments. Differences of opinion are sharper. For
the first time since several organizations began to function where
only two had functioned before, there emerges what seems to be a
difference in goals.

Heretofore there were some differences in methods and in
emphases, but none in ultimate goals. The end was always to be the
inclusion of the Negro American, without racial discrimination, as a
full-fledged equal in all phases of American citizenship. The targets
were whatever barriers, crude or subtle, which blocked the
attainment of that goal.

There has now emerged, first, a strident and threatening challenge
to a strategy widely employed by civil rights groups, namely,
nonviolence. One organization, which has been meeting in Baltimore, has passed a resolution declaring for defense of themselves by
Negro citizens if they are attacked.

We freed seventy-nine Arkansas sharecroppers in a four-year court
battle beginning in 1919. They had returned gunfire directed at a
meeting they were holding in a church.

We employed the late Clarence Darrow in 1926 to defend a man
and his family when a member of a mob threatening his newly-
purchased Detroit home was shot and killed. The NAACP has
subscribed to nonviolence as a humane as well as a practical
necessity in the realities of the American scene, but we have never
required this as a deep personal commitment of our members. We
never signed a pact either on paper or in our hearts to turn the other
cheek forever and ever when we were assaulted.

But neither have we couched a policy of manly resistance in such

Roy Wilkins' speech was given in Los Angeles on July 5, 1966. It is
reprinted by his permission.

a way that our members and supporters felt compelled to maintain themselves in an armed state, ready to retaliate instantly and in kind whenever attacked. We venture the observation that such a publicized posture could serve to stir counter-planning, counter-action and possible conflict. If carried out literally as instant retaliation, in cases adjudged by aggrieved persons to have been grossly unjust, this policy could produce—in extreme situations—lynchings, or, in better-sounding phraseology, private, vigilante vengeance.

Moreover, in attempting to substitute for derelict law enforcement machinery, the policy entails the risk of a broader, more indiscriminate crackdown by law officers, under the ready-made excuse of restoring law and order.

It seems reasonable to assume that proclaimed protective violence is as likely to encourage counter-violence as it is to discourage violent persecution.

But the more serious division in the civil rights movement is the one posed by a word formulation that implies clearly a difference in goals.

No matter how endlessly they try to explain it, the term "black power" means anti-white power. In a racially pluralistic society, the concept, the formation and the exercise of an ethnically-tagged power, means opposition to other ethnic powers, just as the term "white supremacy" means subjection of all non-white people. In the black-white relationship, it has to mean that every other ethnic power is the rival and the antagonist of "black power." It has to mean "going-it-alone." It has to mean separatism.

Now, separatism, whether on the rarefied debate level of "black power" or on the wishful level of a secessionist Freedom City in Watts, offers a disadvantaged minority little except the chance to shrivel and die.

The only possible dividend of "black power" is embodied in its offer to millions of frustrated and deprived and persecuted black people of a solace, a tremendous psychological lift, quite apart from its political and economic implications.

Ideologically it dictates "up with black and down with white" in precisely the same fashion that South Africa reverses that slogan.

It is a reverse Mississippi, a reverse Hitler, a reverse Ku Klux Klan.

If these were evil in our judgment, what virtue can be claimed for black over white? If, as some proponents claim, this concept instills pride of race, cannot this pride be taught without preaching hatred or supremacy based upon race?

Though it be clarified and clarified again, "black power" in the quick, uncritical and highly emotional adoption it has received from some segments of a beleaguered people can mean in the end only black death. Even if, through some miracle, it should be enthroned briefly in an isolated area, the human spirit, which knows no color or geography or time, would die a little, leaving for wiser and stronger and more compassionate men the painful beating back to the upward trail.

We of the NAACP will have none of this. We have fought it too long. It is the ranging of race against race on the irrelevant basis of skin color. It is the father of hatred and the mother of violence.

It is the wicked fanaticism which has swelled our tears, broken our bodies, squeezed our hearts and taken the blood of our black and white loved ones. It shall not now poison our forward march.

We seek, therefore, as we have sought these many years, the inclusion of Negro Americans in the nation's life, not their exclusion. This is our land, as much so as it is any American's—every square foot of every city and town and village. The task of winning our share is not the easy one of disengagement and flight, but the hard one of work, of short as well as long jumps, of disappointments, and of sweet successes.

In our Fight for Freedom we choose:

1. The power and the majesty of the ballot, the participation of free men in their government, both as voters and as honorable and competent elected and appointed public servants. Year in and year out, the NAACP voter registration work has proceeded. No one except the Federal Government has registered more Negro voters in Mississippi than the NAACP. In six weeks last summer more than twenty thousand new names were added by our workers alone, with additional thousands during an intensive renewal last winter. That work is continuing under the leadership of our Mississippi state president, Dr. Aaron Henry, and of our state director, Charles Evers. Later this month a summer task force will be at work in Louisiana. Already our South Carolina NAACP is busy on registration, as is our Alabama organization.

We are aware that a Louisiana young man, born along the Mississippi border, has been named and confirmed as one of the seven governors of the Federal Reserve Bank. We know that his extraordinary ability finally tipped the scales, but we know also, that, without ballot power, he would not even have been on the scales ready to be tipped.

2. We choose employment for our people—jobs not hidden by

racial labels or euphemisms, not limited by racial restrictions in
access and promotion, whether by employers or organized labor. We
commend a growing number of corporations for expanding their
employment of Negro applicants in technical and professional posts,
but we insist that only the surface has been scratched.

We commend the "good guys" among the trade unions for the
improvement in opportunities and advancement for the Negro
worker, but we condemn the policies of some unions which have
either barred or heavily handicapped the Negro worker. Negro
employment is in a crisis stage. The rate of unemployment ranges
from twice that of whites to four and five times the white rate in
some areas. The answer to the complaint of employers that workers
are not trained is to institute in-plant training, just as they have in
other shortages. The apprentice training stranglehold must be
broken, the racially separate seniority lines, the still-persisting
segregated local and the remaining crude segregation in plant
facilities must be abolished. The demonstrations before the U.S.
Steel Corporation offices and plants under the cooperative
leadership of Dr. John Nixon, our Alabama president, and Henry
Smith, our Pennsylvania president, had wide and beneficial impact.

The Negro migrant worker, the forgotten man in the employment
picture, must have attention.

In the Watts district of Los Angeles last year the unemployment
rate was more than 30 per cent, a rate higher than that during the
great, nationwide depression of the nineteen-thirties. The Negro
teenage rate is nearly 25 per cent as against 13 per cent for white
teenagers.

Negro employment is a disaster area demanding the strict
enforcement of Title VII of the 1964 Civil Rights Act. The NAACP
has filed more than one thousand complaints with the Equal
Employment Opportunity Commission and will file more until the
law accomplishes what it was enacted to do. As evidence of his
continuing concern, Congressman Augustus Hawkins of Los Angeles
succeeded in having his bill relating to Federal employment passed
by the House as an amendment to Title VII of the 1964 Civil Rights
Act.

3. We choose to combat the color line in housing. In one breath
our opinion-makers decry the existence of the poverty and filth and
crime and degradation of the slums, but in the next they decry
low-cost housing and fair housing laws. Here in California the
hysteria over whether Negro Americans should live in gullies or be

pushed into the sea reached the Proposition 14 stage which the state's highest court has declared unconstitutional. But who cares about the Constitution when a Negro might be enabled to move into the neighborhood? One could think black Americans were men from Mars. Instead, we have been here, side by side with the white folks (some of whom just got here), for 345 years.

They tell us to work hard and save our money, to go to school and prepare ourselves, to be "responsible," to rear and educate our children in a wholesome and directed family atmosphere, to achieve, to "get up in the world."

After we do all this, they look us in the eye and bar us from renting or buying a home that matches our achievements and one in keeping with our aspirations for further advancement.

Some public officials, including mayors of cities, and many candidates for election to public office are not above public double talk and private single talk on this issue. Any candidate who orates about basic Americanism or "the American way," but who hems and haws over fair housing legislation, is no friend of the Negro citizen.

The Administration's civil rights bill of 1966 with its vital section barring discrimination in the rental or sale of housing must be enacted with the amendment, already inserted by the committee, providing for administrative redress as well as court action.

Your Congressmen and Senators are at home until July 11 celebrating Independence Day—Freedom Day for the United States. See them or have your branch officers back home see them in person. Urge them to rub some freedom off on twenty million loyal Americans by voting for a strong civil rights bill. Of course the section on punishing in the Federal courts those who attack civil rights workers must pass. And we must have indemnification for victims.

4. Most of all, we choose to secure unsegregated, high quality public education for ourselves and our children. A new report, made public only last week, is a jolt for anyone who thought the 1954 Supreme Court decision or subsequent legislation solved the problem.

The report says officially and professionally what we have contended all along: that predominately Negro schools are inferior to those attended largely by whites. Also that the achievement gap widens between the first grade and the twelfth. In other words, the longer our children attend racially segregated schools, the farther they fall behind white children.

And, lest the non-Southerners feel smug, the report found that segregation for both whites and Negroes is more complete in the South, but "is extensive in other regions where the Negro population is concentrated: the urban North, Midwest and West."

The Federal Government, whose Office of Education has made some strong statements, must follow up with a strong enforcement of Title VI of the 1964 law. The empty promises of school officials and the defiance of the whole State of Alabama must not be accepted meekly by Federal officials. The furor over the guidelines issued by HEW is another version of the Dixie bluff on race which has worked so well for so many decades. The guidelines are mild. They are legal and not illegal as Governor Wallace proclaimed to his state's educators. They ask the Southerners to do what is for them a strange thing: obey the school desegregation law. On this point the Federal Government must not yield. The Attorney General and the Department of Justice must back up resolutely the legality of Federal action. There can be no temporizing.

Outside the South the call is for unrelenting activity to wipe out de facto school segregation. Boston, Massachusetts, has proved to be the Mississippi of the North. In fact, in fairness to Mississippi and in consideration of the starting points and traditions of the two places, Boston is *below* Mississippi on this issue. The details, the traps, the methods and the progress will be covered in workshop discussions, but here it must be said that before we can get jobs to earn increased income to buy and rent better homes, before we can contribute to the enrichment of our nation, we must have free access to quality education.

The man who shoots and burns and drowns us is surely our enemy; but so is he who cripples our children for life with inferior public education.

5. We also choose to wrestle with the complex problems of urban life, all of which include an attitude toward and a treatment of millions of Negro citizens. The solution of urban problems will become the solution of living in the last third of our century since more than 70 per cent of Americans now live in urban communities.

If it has been asked once, it has been asked a hundred times: Are we going to have a long, hot summer? The answer has many facets, some extremely complex and difficult. But one quick answer is that the police everywhere can make or break urban racial tensions by their conduct toward minority group citizens.

Last summer you had here an upheaval that shook the world. To many of us who looked from afar, it appeared to be a wild, senseless rampage of hate and destruction. But that was far from the whole truth.

There was powder in Watts, piled up and packed down through the years: wide-scale unemployment, both adult and teenage, slum housing, crowded schools, non-existent health facilities, inadequate transportation and—the Parker police attitude. Everyone was suspect and everyone was subject to harassment in one form or another. The community smoldered under the peculiar brand that police place upon a whole section with their constant sirens, their contemptuous searches, their rough talk, their ready guns and their general "Godalmightiness."

The lesson they and city officials have learned from last year is to seek not correction and improvement, but still more repression. Mayor Yorty and whoever writes his scripts testified in Sacramento in support of a so-called riot-control bill.

The only thing one has to remember about this bill is that it would allow a policeman to judge whether an utterance or an act is an incitement to riot! On his own judgment he could arrest or club or otherwise deter—or shoot—a person whom he (not the law or the courts) deemed to be an inciter of riot. Down the drain goes freedom of speech and down, too, possibly, goes a life.

The McCone Report on the 1965 riot called for "costly and extreme" remedies for Watts, undertaken with a "revolutionary attitude." The answer of the City of Los Angeles was to vote down a hospital bond issue. The answer of Mayor Yorty and of his man, Chief Parker, is a trampling-tough riot-control bill which, if enacted, would loose the police, almost without restraint, upon a populace sick to death—literally—of race control. To blot out any remaining fitful light, one of the gubernatorial candidates, full of disavowals, is the darling of those ultra-conservatives who believe in iron control of what they call "violence in the streets"—their code name for Negroes.

If this is the best that a great city can bring to a hard urban problem, one largely of its own making, then God pity both the whites and the Negroes!

We have no panacea for all these problems. We do not proclaim that what we declare here this week is going to change the course of the whole civil rights movement. We do not know all the answers to the George Wallace problem in Alabama, the James Eastland problem in Mississippi, or to the Boston, Massachusetts, school committee and its Louise Day Hicks problem. We certainly don't know the answers to foreign policy and to tax and interest rate puzzlers.

But in this unsettled time when shifts are the order of the day and when change is in the air, we can sail our NAACP ship "steady as she goes," with more drive to the turbines, more skill at the wheel, but no fancy capers for the sake of capers.

We can follow down into each community the really advanced blueprint of the White House Conference "To Fulfill These Rights," which covered four principal areas: economic security and welfare, education, housing, and the administration of justice.

We can expand and point up the community services of our NAACP branches, each of which is, in reality, a citizenship clinic. Just as medical clinics need specialists to cure physical ills, so our branch clinics should recruit volunteer specialists to diagnose and minister to social ills.

We must involve people in the communities in the solution of our problem—not limiting ourselves to our church or lodge or club group.

We must keep the pressure on our local and state education systems through the employment of every legitimate technique: protests, surveys, discussions, demonstrations, picketing and negotiation. Nothing should be overlooked in fighting for better education. Be persistent and ornery; this will be good for the lethargic educational establishment and will aid the whole cause of public education.

Our branches are at work in their territories. In Baltimore the NAACP won a case against the police commissioner which the Fourth Circuit Court of Appeals declared revealed the most flagrant police practices ever to come before the court. The Blair County, Pennsylvania, NAACP is busy rooting out the remaining discrimination in public accommodations in Clearfield, Pennsylvania.

The Wilmington, Ohio, NAACP has a program for tutoring adults and drop-outs and has recruited college professors and students and textbooks to make the project effective. The Bay City, Michigan, NAACP also has a tutorial program under way as well as continuous work on industrial employment practices and housing. The Stillwater, Oklahoma, NAACP is active on a child care center project and on high school desegregation.

And the Montgomery County, West Virginia, NAACP, bless its

heart, is 112 per cent above last year in membership and 500 per cent above last year in funds raised.

Thirty one branches found time and funds to be present at the Meredith march rally in Jackson, Mississippi, even though the Association, at the last minute, was insulted by the barring of Charles Evers as an NAACP spokesman.

This is only part of the chronicle of "steady as she goes." In a world where the Mayor of Los Angeles is yelling "riot control," where Rhodesia says "never!" to black representation while in America SNCC raises the chant of black power, where the Federal Government at long last is committed, but both the far right and the far left offer vocal and vicious objection, someone has to drive the long haul toward the group goal of Negro Americans and the larger ideal of our young nation.

Our objective is basically as it was laid down in 1909 by the interracial founders of our NAACP. Back there William Lloyd Garrison expressed the strong feeling that the first NAACP conference "will utter no uncertain sound on any point affecting the vital subject. No part of it is too delicate for plain speech. The republican experiment is at stake, every tolerated wrong to the Negro reacting with double force upon white citizens guilty of faithlessness to their brothers."

As it was then, so it is today. The republican experiment is at stake in 1966. More than that, the dream of a brotherhood in equality and justice is imperiled.

Our fraternity tonight, as it was then, is the fraternity of man, not the white, or brown, or yellow, or black man, but man.

7

The Pattern
of a Speech

CRITICAL INTRODUCTION

Common Efforts for the Common Good: Patterning in the Speeches of Jefferson and Churchill

Moving audiences to work in harmony to achieve common ends: Throughout history speakers have sought to do this. Indeed, it has been argued that rhetoric is one of the principal methods of submerging differences in an effort to achieve shared goals. The speeches by Thomas Jefferson, third President of the United States, and Winston Churchill, Prime Minister of Great Britain, were both directed toward such an end. The organizational patterns employed in each of their speeches served to promote their similar purposes.

The fierce political campaign that preceded Jefferson's election in 1800 was characterized by the fears of Federalists that Jefferson's Republican party was committed to the sanguine principles of the French Revolution. The tumultuous events in France at the end of the eighteenth century had made conservatives extremely suspicious of popular rule. Because Jefferson and his supporters were committed to the extension of democracy, Federalists were inclined to view them as the American counterparts of the French Jacobins. Bitter hostilities had been engendered. As the new President prepared to take the oath of office on March 4, 1801, it could not be denied that political wounds were fresh and potentially deep divisions among the citizens of the young republic existed.

The inauguration of a President is a formal occasion, and the address given is traditionally a broad statement of principles rather than a detailed enunciation of specific programs. So it was at the time of Jefferson's inauguration. This particular occasion then called for a speech that sketched the general outlines of the new President's philosophy, and took into account strong feelings of political rivalry and suspicion.

Jefferson set out in his introduction, after a few brief words of gratitude and recognition of the honor and the burden of the Presidency, to suggest the theme of unity he would presently develop. He touched on the great potential of the "rising nation," and, with reference to commerce, reminded his listeners that they must deal "with nations who feel power and forget right." The development of domestic resources would obviously be accomplished only by joint efforts; potential enemies abroad would demand united action at home. Addressing the legislators in his audience, Jefferson specifically called upon them for help, stressing the mutual interdependence of the branches of government as provided for, and, by implication thus united by a common devotion to, the Constitution. The introduction concluded with a direct reference to unity, which served to provide a transition to the main point: a call for "support which may enable us to steer with safety the vessel in which we are all embarked amidst the conflicting elements of a troubled world." The metaphor of a ship at sea is plain, for only the cooperation between captain and crew would save it from foundering in stormy waters.

This metaphor, then, served as an excellent transition to the body of the speech in which Jefferson's first main point was developed: In spite of all political differences, "all will, of course, arrange themselves under the will of the law, and unite in common efforts for the common good." Given the feelings of uneasiness and distrust engendered by the election campaign, it was doubtless wise that the new President should first address himself to this principle. For it was necessary to establish his dedication to basic unity before undertaking to outline his own political philosophy. To those who opposed him or feared him, Jefferson held out the olive branch. His stress of commonalities must have been directed toward allaying hostility. He reminded his listeners, as he developed the point, that free debate, no matter how hotly engaged in, was ultimately decided by "the voice of the nation." But, lest his opponents fear that losing an election meant losing their rights, Jefferson was quick to affirm "that though the will of the majority is in all cases to prevail, that will to be rightful must be reasonable; that the minority possesses their equal rights, which equal law must protect, and to violate would be oppression." With this assurance in mind, Jefferson then called upon his audience to "unite with one mind," and to restore "harmony and affection."

The President well knew that the events in France had sharply divided American opinion. He referred directly to the throes and convulsions of the "ancient world" and the attendant differences expressed as to the "measures of safety" to be pursued in the United States. "But," Jefferson asserted, "every difference of opinion is not a difference of principle." The next section of the speech is devoted to reinforcing the unity theme by pointing out the basic premises of government to which all parties held. "We are all Republicans, we are all Federalists," because we all believe in the union and representative government. During the Adams Administration the Alien and Sedition laws had curtailed free speech and criticism of the government. Jefferson and his followers were opposed to those laws even though they had not agreed with some of the more revolutionary sentiments expressed by dissidents. Even as he pleaded for unity, the President affirmed the right to disagree in one of the most memorable and fundamental statements on the foundation of American liberty: "If there be any among us who would wish to dissolve this Union or to change its republican form, let them stand undisturbed as monuments of the safety with which error of opinion may be tolerated where reason is left free to combat it." Jefferson recognized that some, "honest men" he called them in conciliatory spirit, were unsure of the efficacy of republican government. Then he urged his audience not to "abandon a government which has so far kept us free and firm," and expressed his belief that, "on the contrary, [this is] the strongest Government on earth." Jefferson concluded his development of the initial theme of unity and shared principles with the historical allusion to the failure of monarchical government.

Jefferson's transition to his next point was effected by building on all that had gone before. "Let us, then, with courage and confidence pursue our own Federal and Republican principles, our attachment to union and representative government." The long enumeration of all the advantages of the young republic was an indirect method of development of the principal point that Jefferson next made: With all the natural endowments America enjoyed, only a "wise and frugal government" was necessary to "close the circle of our felicities." This point was an excellent bridge between the unity theme and the specific enumeration of "the essential principles of our Government" which would "shape [Jefferson's] Administration." What then followed was a long list, without elaboration, of those principles, "the creed of our political faith." To his audience these were hardly controversial points, and they tended to reaffirm the important contention of the earlier section of the speech that differences of opinion were not differences of principle.

With a final call for support, a pledge to do all in his power "to retain the good opinion of those who have bestowed it in advance, to conciliate that of others by doing them all the good in my power, and to be instrumental to the happiness and freedom of all," and a prayer that "that Infinite Power which rules the destiny of the universe" may guide the country's leaders, Thomas Jefferson concluded his Inaugural Address.

It may be seen that the pattern of Jefferson's speech is clearly designed to enhance his essential purpose within the context of audience and occasion. The primacy of the unity theme is apparent as is the skill with which the President wove together his ideas.

On December 8, 1941, the United States entered World War II. For two years Great Britain had been struggling, virtually single-handed, against Nazi Germany. Some American aid had been given to Britain, but now the full potential might of the United States was joined with hers against the Axis powers. As Prime Minister, Winston Churchill had rallied the British people; his speeches given to the House of Commons during the days of trial and defeat are among the most powerful and moving in the English language. Soon after the United States entered the conflict, Churchill traveled to Washington to meet with President Roosevelt. He was invited to address a joint session of Congress on December 26.

Churchill's task was to promote the new spirit of unity and cooperation between the two democracies. The Prime Minister clearly saw that the war would be long and hard; but he saw, too, that disaster was no longer likely, that the long road ahead was an uphill one. Furthermore, as his speech definitely indicates, he hoped to lay the foundations for a long-lasting alliance between the two English-speaking countries.

Churchill developed four main ideas: (1) The United States and Great Britain share a common heritage; (2) that while the United States was justifiably confident, a long and difficult war was to be expected; (3) events already showed that victory would surely come; and, (4) a strong and lasting British-American alliance was necessary not only for the prosecution of the war, but also for the mutual benefit of the two countries in the future.

As the overall pattern of this speech is examined, it appears that Churchill, rather than beginning with his most crucial proposition (that a continuing and strong Anglo-American alliance was desirable), led more indirectly to it. The principal ideas that the Prime Minister developed were expertly sequenced. The first, that the United States and Britain shared a common heritage, provided a perfect introduction for what was to follow. Churchill began with a personal statement of this heritage and moved to a discussion of institutional and idealistic bonds. Churchill's father, Lord Randolph Churchill, married the beautiful New York socialite Jennie Jerome, so that Winston himself was part American. After the brief reference to his "American forebears," Churchill mentioned his own long career in the House of Commons, and his father's famous advice to "Trust the people." Thus Churchill was able to remind his audience of the shared values of democracy and representative government, and to reach the conclusion: "Therefore I have been in full harmony all my life with the tides which have flowed on both sides of the Atlantic against privilege and monopoly" and to state as a common ideal, "the Gettysburg ideal of 'government of the people, by the people, and for the people.' "

Explaining that he had come to the United States to consult with President Roosevelt on the conduct of the war, Churchill provided a transition to his next main idea, that the United States was confident of the final outcome of the long war ahead. Even as he elaborated on this point, Churchill injected expressions of British-American commonalities. "We in Britain had the same feeling in our darkest days," he told his audience in reference to Washington's "Olympian fortitude." And the "youth of Britain and America" were contrasted with the youth of the enemy countries. Churchill did not choose to elaborate on this point in much detail. The function of this section of the speech seemed to be to compliment the United States on its firm resolve and to remind the American Congress and people that a quick and easy victory was not possible, that, on the contrary, Britain and the United States were "at a disadvantage which only time, courage, and straining, untiring exertions can correct."

The essence of this warning was carried on as Churchill proceeded through his next major idea, that the tide had begun to turn and the long, hard exertions would lead ultimately to triumph; this section of the speech is basically a more detailed review of the war situation. Churchill enunciated a series of general statements that stressed his conviction that the entrance into the war of the United States, with its great industrial potential, would "produce results in war power beyond anything that has yet been seen or foreseen in the dictator states." It is clear that to Churchill the total commitment of "the English-speaking world" made victory inevitable. Assuring his audience that "we are the masters of our fate; that the task which has been set for us is not above our strength, and that its pangs and toils are not beyond our endurance," Churchill turned to an assessment of the specific events in Europe, North Africa, and Asia. As he outlined hopeful signs in all quarters of the globe, Churchill took every opportunity to refer to British-American unity: the tanks and aircraft in Libya were British and American, the "best tidings of all" were that the United States had "drawn the sword for freedom, and cast away the scabbard," the United States had already sent "munitions for the defense of the British Isles." Coming finally to the war with Japan, which had so recently begun, Churchill hammered home the invincibility of the two allied powers: "Now that we are together, now that we are linked in a righteous comradeship of arms, now that our two considerable nations, each in perfect unity, have joined all their life energies in a common resolve, a new scene opens upon which a steady light will glow and brighten." After ridiculing the folly of Japan in declaring war on both the British Empire and the United States simultaneously, Churchill moved to his final point as he declared, "Members of the Senate and Members of the House of Representatives, I turn for one moment more from the turmoil and convulsions of the present to the broader spaces of the future."

Churchill had reached the climax of his speech. From the common heritage, through the common efforts against the common foe, Churchill had come to the plea for an enduring alliance. Surely this was the essential point of the speech. There was no doubt about the existing cooperation between the two countries faced by the same powerful enemy. From the present starting point ("Here we are together, facing a group of mighty foes who seek our ruin. Here we are together, defending all that to freemen is dear.") Churchill hoped to cement a lasting unity. He reminded Congress that joint action in the past might have prevented the present war, "If we had kept together," much would have been different. "Prodigious hammer strokes have been needed to bring us together today," and the Prime Minister earnestly sought to keep the new relationship viable in the long future. His final statement epitomized Churchill's hope and truly culminated the carefully developed speech: "I avow my faith and hope, sure and inviolate, that in days to come the British and American peoples will for their own safety and for the good of all, walk together side by side in majesty, in justice, and in peace." The arrangement of ideas, their natural flow from one to the next, all contributing to the purpose and suitable to the occasion, leading to the climactic conclusion, affords an excellent example of appropriate and careful patterning.

THOMAS JEFFERSON

FIRST INAUGURAL ADDRESS

Friends and fellow-citizens, called upon to undertake the duties of the first executive office of our country, I avail myself of the presence of that portion of my fellow-citizens which is here assembled to express my grateful thanks for the favor with which they have been pleased to look toward me, to declare a sincere consciousness that the task is above my talents, and that I approach it with those anxious and awful presentiments which the greatness of the charge and the weakness of my powers so justly inspire. A rising nation, spread over a wide and fruitful land, traversing all the seas with the rich productions of their industry, engaged in commerce with nations who feel power and forget right, advancing rapidly to destinies beyond the reach of mortal eye—when I contemplate these transcendent objects, and see the honor, the happiness, and the hopes of this beloved country committed to the issue, and the auspices of this day, I shrink from the contemplation, and humble

Thomas Jefferson's speech was given in Washington, D.C., on March 4, 1801. It is reprinted from *Inaugural Addresses of the Presidents of the United States,* Washington, D.C.: GPO, 1961, pp. 11–14.

myself before the magnitude of the undertaking. Utterly, indeed, should I despair did not the presence of many whom I here see remind me that in the other high authorities provided by our Constitution I shall find resources of wisdom, of virtue, and of zeal on which to rely under all difficulties. To you, then, gentlemen, who are charged with the sovereign functions of legislation, and to those associated with you, I look with encouragement for that guidance and support which may enable us to steer with safety the vessel in which we are all embarked amidst the conflicting elements of a troubled world.

During the contest of opinion through which we have passed the animation of discussions and of exertions has sometimes worn an aspect which might impose on strangers unused to think freely and to speak and to write what they think; but this being now decided by the voice of the nation, announced according to the rules of the Constitution, all will, of course, arrange themselves under the will of the law, and unite in common efforts for the common good. All, too, will bear in mind this sacred principle, that though the will of the majority is in all cases to prevail, that will to be rightful must be reasonable; that the minority possesses their equal rights, which equal law must protect, and to violate would be oppression. Let us, then, fellow-citizens, unite with one heart and one mind. Let us restore to social intercourse that harmony and affection without which liberty and even life itself are but dreary things. And let us reflect that, having banished from our land that religious intolerance under which mankind so long bled and suffered, we have yet gained little if we countenance a political intolerance as despotic, as wicked, and capable of as bitter and bloody persecutions. During the throes and convulsions of the ancient world, during the agonizing spasms of infuriated man, seeking through blood and slaughter his long-lost liberty, it was not wonderful that the agitation of the billows should reach even this distant and peaceful shore; that this should be more felt and feared by some and less by others, and should divide opinions as to measures of safety. But every difference of opinion is not a difference of principle. We have called by different names brethren of the same principle. We are all Republicans, we are all Federalists. If there be any among us who would wish to dissolve this Union or to change its republican form, let them stand undisturbed as monuments of the safety with which error of opinion may be tolerated where reason is left free to combat it. I know, indeed, that some honest men fear that a republican government can not be strong, that this Government is not strong enough; but would the honest patriot, in the full tide of successful experiment, abandon a government which has so far kept us free and firm on the theoretic and visionary fear that this Government, the world's best hope, may by possibility want energy to preserve itself? I trust not. I believe this, on the contrary, the strongest Government on earth. I believe it the only one where every man, at the call of the law, would fly to the standard of the law, and would meet invasions of the public order as his own personal concern. Sometimes it is said that man can not be trusted with the government of himself. Can he, then, be trusted with the government of others? Or have we found angels in the forms of kings to govern him? Let history answer this question.

Let us, then, with courage and confidence pursue our own Federal and Republican principles, our attachment to union and representative government. Kindly separated by nature and a wide ocean from the exterminating havoc of one quarter of the globe; too high-minded to endure the degradations of the others; possessing a chosen country, with room enough for our descendants to the thousandth and thousandth generation; entertaining a due sense of our equal right to the use of our own faculties, to the acquisitions of our own industry, to honor and confidence from our fellow-citizens, resulting not from birth, but from our actions and their sense of them; enlightened by a benign religion, professed, indeed, and practiced in various forms, yet all of them inculcating honesty, truth, temperance, gratitude, and the love of man; acknowledging and adoring an overruling Providence, which by all its dispensations proves that it delights in the happiness of man here and his greater happiness hereafter—with all these blessings, what more is necessary to make us a happy and a prosperous people? Still one thing more, fellow-citizens—a wise and frugal Government, which shall restrain men from injuring one another, shall leave them otherwise free to regulate their own pursuits of industry and improvement, and shall not take from the mouth of labor the bread it has earned. This is the sum of good government, and this is necessary to close the circle of our felicities.

About to enter, fellow-citizens, on the exercise of duties which comprehend everything dear and valuable to you, it is proper you should understand what I deem the essential principles of our Government, and consequently those which ought to shape its Administration. I will compress them within the narrowest compass they will bear, stating the general principle, but not all its limitations. Equal and exact justice to all men, of whatever state or persuasion, religious or political; peace, commerce, and honest friendship with all nations, entangling alliances with none; the support of the State governments in all their rights, as the most competent administrations for our domestic concerns and the surest bulwarks against antirepublican tendencies; the preservation of the General Government in its whole constitutional vigor, as the sheet anchor of our peace at home and safety abroad; a jealous care of the right of election by the people—a mild and safe corrective of abuses which are lopped by the sword of revolution where peaceable remedies are unprovided; absolute acquiescence in the decisions of the majority, the vital principle of republics, from which is no appeal but to force, the vital principle and immediate parent of despotism; a well-disciplined militia, our best reliance in peace and for the first moments of war, till regulars may relieve them; the supremacy of the civil over the military authority; economy in the public expense, that labor may be lightly burthened; the honest payment of our debts and sacred preservation of the public faith; encouragement of agriculture, and of commerce as its handmaid; the diffusion of information and arraignment of all abuses at the bar of the public reason; freedom of religion; freedom of the press, and freedom of person under the protection of the habeas corpus, and trial by juries impartially selected. These principles form the bright constellation which has gone before us and guided our steps through an age of revolution and reformation. The wisdom of our sages and blood of our heroes have been devoted to their attainment. They should be the creed of our political faith, the text of civic instruction, the touchstone by which to try the services of those we trust; and should we wander from them in moments of error or of alarm, let us hasten to retrace our steps and to regain the road which alone leads to peace, liberty, and safety.

I repair, then, fellow-citizens, to the post you have assigned me. With experience enough in subordinate offices to have seen the difficulties of this the greatest of all, I have learnt to expect that it will rarely fall to the lot of imperfect man to retire from this station with the reputation and the favor which bring him into it. Without pretentions to that high confidence you reposed in our first and greatest revolutionary character, whose preeminent services had entitled him to the first place in his country's love and destined for him the fairest page in the volume of faithful history, I ask so much confidence only as may give firmness and effect to the legal administration of your affairs. I shall often go wrong through defect of judgment. When right, I shall often be thought wrong by those whose positions will not command a view of the whole ground. I ask your indulgence for my own errors, which will never be intentional, and your support against the errors of others, who may condemn what they would not if seen in all its parts. The approbation implied by your suffrage is a great consolation to me for the past, and my future solicitude will be to retain the good opinion of those who have bestowed it in advance, to conciliate that of others by doing them all the good in my power, and to be instrumental to the happiness and freedom of all.

Relying, then, on the patronage of your good will, I advance with obedience to the work, ready to retire from it whenever you become sensible how much better choice it is in your power to make. And may that Infinite Power which rules the destinies of the universe lead our councils to what is best, and give them a favorable issue for your peace and prosperity.

WINSTON S. CHURCHILL

ADDRESS TO THE CONGRESS

Members of the Senate and of the House of Representatives of the United States, I feel greatly honored that you should have invited me to enter the United States Senate Chamber and address the representatives of both branches of Congress.

The fact that my American forebears have for so many generations played their part in the life of the United States, and that here I am, an Englishman, welcomed in your midst, makes this experience one of the most moving and thrilling in my life, which is already long and has not been entirely uneventful. [Laughter.]

I wish indeed that my mother, whose memory I cherish across the vale of years, could have been here to see. By the way, I cannot help

Winston S. Churchill's speech was given in Washington, D.C., on December 26, 1941. It is reprinted from the *Congressional Record, Senate* December 26, 1941, pp. 10117–10119.

reflecting that if my father had been American and my mother British, instead of the other way round, I might have got here on my own. [Laughter and applause.] In that case, this would not have been the first time you would have heard my voice. In that case, I should not have needed any invitation; but, if I had, it is hardly likely that it would have been unanimous. [Laughter.] So perhaps things are better as they are.

I may confess, however, that I do not feel quite like a fish out of water in a legislative assembly where English is spoken. I am a child of the House of Commons. I was brought up in my father's house to believe in democracy, "Trust the people"—that was his message. I used to see him cheered at meetings and in the streets by crowds of workingmen away back in those aristocratic Victorian days when, as Disraeli said, the world was for the few, and for the very few. Therefore I have been in full harmony all my life with the tides which have flowed on both sides of the Atlantic against privilege and monopoly and have steered confidently toward the Gettysburg ideal of "government of the people, by the people, for the people." [Applause.]

I owe my advancement entirely to the House of Commons, whose servant I am. In my country, as in yours, public men are proud to be the servants of the state, and would be ashamed to be its masters. On any day, if they thought the people wanted it, the House of Commons could by a simple vote remove me from my office. But I am not worrying about it at all. [Laughter.] As a matter of fact, I am sure they will approve very highly of my journey here—for which I obtained the King's permission—in order to meet the President of the United States [applause] and to arrange with him for all that mapping out of our military plans, and for all those intimate meetings of the high officers of the armed services of both countries which are indispensable to the successful prosecution of the war.

I should like to say, first of all, how much I have been impressed and encouraged by the breadth of view and sense of proportion which I have found in all quarters over here to which I have had access. Anyone who did not understand the size and solidity of the foundations of the United States might easily have expected to find an excited, disturbed, self-centered atmosphere, with all minds fixed upon the novel, startling, and painful episodes of sudden war as they hit America. After all, the United States has been attacked and set upon by three most powerfully armed dictator states, the greatest military power in Europe, and the greatest military power in Asia.

Japan, Germany, and Italy have all declared and are making war upon you, and a quarrel is opened which can only end in their overthrow or yours. But here in Washington, in these memorable days, I have found an Olympian fortitude which, far from being based upon complacency, is only the mask of an inflexible purpose and the proof of a sure and well-grounded confidence in the final outcome. [Applause.] We in Britain had the same feeling in our darkest days. We, too, were sure that in the end all would be well.

You do not, I am certain, underrate the severity of the ordeal to which you and we have still to be subjected. The forces ranged against us are enormous; they are bitter; they are ruthless. The wicked men and their factions who have launched their peoples on the path of war and conquest know that they will be called to terrible account if they can not beat down by force of arms the peoples they have assailed. They will stop at nothing. They have a vast accumulation of war weapons of all kinds; they have highly-trained and disciplined armies, navies, and air services; they have plans and designs which have long been contrived and matured; they will stop at nothing that violence or treachery can suggest.

It is quite true that on our side our resources in manpower and in materials are far greater than theirs; but only a portion of your resources are as yet mobilized and developed, and we have both of us much to learn in the cruel art of war. We have, therefore, without doubt, a time of tribulation before us. In this time some ground will be lost which it will be hard and costly to regain. Many disappointments and unpleasant surprises await us. Many of them will afflict us before the full marshalling of our latent and total power can be accomplished.

For the best part of 20 years the youth of Britain and American have been taught that war was evil, which is true, and that it would never come again, which has been proved false.

For the best part of 20 years the youth of Germany, Japan, and Italy have been taught that aggressive war is the noblest duty of the citizen, and that it should be begun as soon as the necessary weapons and organization have been made. We have performed the duties and tasks of peace. They have plotted and planned for war. This naturally has placed us in Britain, and now places you in the United States, at a disadvantage which only time, courage, and straining, untiring exertions can correct.

We have, indeed, to be thankful that so much time has been granted to us. If Germany had tried to invade the British Isles after the French collapse in June 1940, and if Japan had declared war on the British Empire and the United States at about the same date, no one can say what disasters and agonies might not have been our lot. But now, at the end of December 1941, our transformation from easygoing peace to total-war efficiency has made very great progress. The broad flow of munitions in Great Britain has already begun. Immense strides have been made in the conversion of American industry to military purposes, and now that the United States is at war, it is possible for orders to be given every day which a year or 18 months hence will produce results in war power beyond anything which has yet been seen or foreseen in the dictator states. Provided that every effort is made, that nothing is kept back, that the whole manpower, brainpower, virility, valour, and civic virtue of the English-speaking world, with all its galaxy of loyal, friendly, or associated communities and states, are bent unremittingly to the simple but supreme task, I think it would be reasonable to hope that the end of 1942 will see us quite definitely in a better position than we are now [applause], and that the year 1943 will enable us to assume the initiative upon an ample scale. [Applause.]

Some people may be startled or momentarily depressed when, like your President, I speak of a long and a hard war. Our peoples would rather know the truth, sombre though it be; and, after all, when we are doing the noblest work in the world, not only defending our hearths and homes but the cause of freedom in every land, the question of whether deliverance comes in 1942, or 1943, or 1944, falls into its proper place in the grand proportions of human history. [Applause.] Sure I am that this day, now, we are the masters of our fate; that the task which has been set for us is not above our strength, and that its pangs and toils are not beyond our endurance. As long as we have faith in our cause and unconquerable will power, salvation will not be denied us. In the words of the Psalmist: "He shall not be afraid of evil tidings: his heart is fixed, trusting in the Lord."

Not all the tidings will be evil. On the contrary, mighty strokes of war have already been dealt against the enemy. The glorious defense of their native soil by the Russian Armies and people have inflicted wounds upon the Nazi tyranny and system which have bitten deep, and will fester and inflame not only in the Nazi body but in the Nazi mind. [Applause.]

The boastful Mussolini [laughter] has crumpled already. He is now but a lackey and serf, the merest utensil of his master's will.

[Laughter and applause.] He has inflicted great suffering and wrong upon his own industrious people. He has been stripped of all his African empire. Abyssinia has been liberated. Our armies of the east, which were so weak and ill equipped at the moment of French desertion, now control all the regions from Teheran to Benghazi, and from Aleppo to Cyprus and the sources of the Nile. [Applause.]

For many months we devoted ourselves to preparing to take the offensive in Libya. The very considerable battle which has been proceeding for the last 6 weeks in the desert has been most fiercely fought on both sides. Owing to the difficulties of supply on the desert flank we were never able to bring numerically equal forces to bear upon the enemy. Therefore we had to rely upon a superiority in the numbers and quality of tanks and aircraft, British and American. Aided by these, for the first time we have fought the enemy with equal weapons. For the first time we have made the Hun feel the sharp edge of those tools with which he has enslaved Europe. The armed force of the enemy in Cyrenaica amounted to 150,000 men, of whom about a third were Germans. General Auchinleck set out to destroy totally that armed force; and I have every reason to believe that his aim will be fully accomplished. [Applause.]

I am so glad to be able to place before you, Members of the Senate and of the House of Representatives, at this moment when you are entering the war, proof that, with proper weapons and proper organization, we are able to beat the life out of the savage Nazi. [Applause.] What Hitler is suffering in Libya is only a sample and a foretaste of what we must give him and his accomplices wherever this war shall lead us, in every quarter of the globe.

There are good tidings also from blue water. The life line of supplies which joins our two nations across the ocean, without which all might fail, is flowing steadily and freely, in spite of all the enemy can do. It is a fact that the British Empire, which many thought 18 months ago was broken and ruined, is now incomparably stronger and is growing stronger with every month. [Applause.]

Lastly, if you will forgive me for saying it, to me the best tiding of all, the United States—united as never before—has drawn the sword for Freedom, and cast away the scabbard. [Applause.]

All these tremendous facts have led the subjugated peoples of Europe to lift up their heads again in hope. They have put aside forever the shameful temptation of resigning themselves to the conqueror's will. Hope has returned to the hearts of scores of millions of men and women, and with that hope there burns the flame of anger against the brutal, corrupt invader, and still more fiercely burn the fires of hatred and contempt for the filthy Quislings whom he has suborned. In a dozen famous ancient states, now prostrate under the Nazi yoke, the masses of the people, all classes and creeds, await the hour of liberation, when they, too, will be able once again to play their part and strike their blows like men. That hour will strike, and its solemn peal will proclaim that the night is passed and that the dawn has come.

The onslaught upon us, so long and so secretly planned by Japan, has presented both our countries with grievous problems for which we could not be fully prepared. If people ask me, as they have a right to ask me in England, "Why is it that you have not got ample equipment of modern aircraft and army weapons of all kinds in Malaya and in the East Indies" I can only point to the victories General Auchinleck has gained in the Libyan campaign. Had we diverted and dispersed our gradually growing resources between Libya and Malaya, we should have been found wanting in both theatres. If the United States has been found at a disadvantage at various points in the Pacific Ocean, we know well that it is to no small extent because of the aid which you have been giving to us in munitions for the defense of the British Isles and for the Libyan campaign, and, above all, because of your help in the battle of the Atlantic, upon which all depends, and which has in consequence been successfully and prosperously maintained.

Of course, it would have been much better, I freely admit, if we had had enough resources of all kinds to be at full strength at all threatened points; but, considering how slowly and reluctantly we brought ourselves to large-scale preparations, and how long such preparations take, we had no right to expect to be in such a fortunate position. The choice of how to dispose of our hitherto limited resources had to be made by Britain in time of war, and by the United States in time of peace; and I believe that history will pronounce that upon the whole—and it is upon the whole that these matters must be judged—the choice made was right.

Now that we are together, now that we are linked in a righteous comradeship of arms, now that our two considerable nations, each in perfect unity, have joined all their life energies in a common resolve, a new scene opens upon which a steady light will glow and brighten.

Many people have been astonished that Japan should, in a single day, have plunged into war against the United States and the British Empire. We all wonder why, if this dark design, with all its labourious and intricate preparations, had been so long filling their secret minds, they did not choose our moment of weakness 18 months ago. Viewed quite dispassionately, in spite of the losses we have suffered and the further punishment we shall have to take, it certainly appears to be an irrational act. It is, of course, only prudent to assume that they have made very careful calculation and think they see their way through. Nevertheless, there may be another explanation.

We know that for many years past the policy of Japan has been dominated by secret societies of subaltern and junior officers of the Army and Navy who have enforced their will upon successive Japanese cabinets and parliaments by the assassination of any Japanese statesman who opposed or who did not sufficiently further their aggressive policy. It may be that these societies, dazzled and dizzy with their own schemes of aggression and the prospect of early victories, have forced their country, against its better judgment, into war. They have certainly embarked upon a very considerable undertaking [laughter] ; for, after the outrages they have committed upon us at Pearl Harbor, in the Pacific Islands, in the Philippines, in Malaya, and the Dutch East Indies, they must now know that the stakes for which they have decided to play are mortal. When we consider the resources of the United States and the British Empire, compared to those of Japan, when we remember those of China, which has so long and valiantly withstood invasion [great applause] , and when also we observe the Russian menace which hangs over Japan, it becomes still more difficult to reconcile Japanese action with prudence, or even with sanity. What kind of people do they think we are? Is it possible they do not realize that we shall never cease to persevere against them until they have been taught a lesson which they and the world will never forget? [Prolonged applause.]

Members of the Senate and Members of the House of Representative, I turn for one moment more from the turmoil and convulsions of the present to the broader spaces of the future.

Here we are together, facing a group of mighty foes who seek our ruin. Here we are together, defending all that to freemen is dear. Twice in a single generation the catastrophe of world war has fallen upon us; twice in our lifetimes has the long arm of Fate reached out across the oceans to bring the United States into the forefront of the battle. If we had kept together after the last war; if we had taken common measures for our safety, this renewal of the curse need never have fallen upon us. [Applause.] Do we not owe it to ourselves, to our children, to tormented mankind, to make sure that these catastrophes do not engulf us for the third time?

It has been proved that pestilences may break out in the Old World which carry their destructive ravages into the New World, from which, once they are afoot, the New World cannot by any means escape. Duty and prudence alike command, first, that the germ centres of hatred and revenge should be constantly and vigilantly surveyed and treated in good time; and, secondly, that an adequate organization should be set up to make sure that the pestilence can be controlled at its earliest beginnings before it spreads and rages throughout the entire earth. [Applause.]

Five or six years ago it would have been easy, without shedding a drop of blood, for the United States and Great Britain to have insisted on fulfillment of the disarmament clauses of the treaties which Germany signed after the Great War. That also would have been the opportunity for assuring to Germans those raw materials which we declared in the Atlantic Charter should not be denied to any nation, victor or vanquished.

Prodigious hammer strokes have been needed to bring us together today; or, if you will allow me to use other language, I will say that he must, indeed, have a blind soul who cannot see that some great purpose and design is being worked out here below, of which we have the honour to be the faithful servants.

It is not given to us to peer into the mysteries of the future; still I avow my hope and faith, sure and inviolate, that in days to come the British and American peoples will for their own safety and for the good of all, walk together side by side in majesty, in justice, and in peace.

[Prolonged applause, the Members of the Senate and their guests rising.]

8

The Style
of a Speech

**The Language of Dissent:
Style in the Speeches of
Malcolm X and John V. Lindsay**

The 1960s might well be called the decade of dissent. In attempting to solve the problems of the cities, to reexamine and revitalize the university and its role in contemporary America, to gain full equality for the black man, to influence the course of foreign policy, Americans mounted increasingly militant and determined attacks on established policies, programs, and traditions.

Martin Luther King and Roy Wilkins sought to bring freedom and equal opportunity to blacks in ways alluded to in previous essays. The Black Muslim leader, Malcolm X, however, saw past efforts as essentially fruitless, and called for new goals and strategies. He contended that those who interfered with black rights were criminals, that there could be no question of what white men would "give" to black men for blacks were naturally entitled to liberty and complete equality. The black strategy, so the argument ran, could not be based on the assumption that freedom could be granted by whites: Both blacks and whites had to realize that legal and moral rights had to be exercised, no matter what the consequences, and not somehow applied for. If the exercise of these rights led to collision with whites, then the collision must be faced. Malcolm's style reinforced this essential argument as well as contributed to its refinement and development. Further, his style stressed his identity *book*

with the black masses and strengthened his own image as a black spokesman.

Now certainly much could be said about the style of Malcolm X. And even when all *was* said, it would be very difficult to describe his style in such a way that it could be seen to be entirely unique to him. But certainly there are some elements of his language use and choice that exemplify the integrative nature of style—that is, that show how language was used meaningfully in the context of the speaker's argument and audience.

Particularly striking in Malcolm's speech was the use of antithesis. The phrase from which the title of the speech is taken, "the ballot or the bullet," was repeated again and again. Such a contrast captures the essence of the speech. Throughout the speech, Malcolm's comparisons and contrasts point up black rights and white failure to recognize those rights. Malcolm argued, for example, that "Whenever you're going after something that belongs to you, anyone who's depriving you of the right to have it is a criminal." He then asserted, "The Supreme Court is on your side." Malcolm pinpointed the paradox: "Now, who is it that opposes you in carrying out the law? The police department itself. . . . They are breaking the law, they are not representatives of the law." Criminals and police, law breakers and law enforcers, are equated. The language clearly augments the argument: To disobey the law enforcers is not to disobey the law; legality has been perverted by the white power structure.

The argument is further elaborated by Malcolm's word choice in describing the white leadership, as well as black leaders who seem to cooperate with them. Malcolm's style contributed greatly to the balancing of the black masses (with Malcolm as a part of them) against the whites and their "Uncle Tom" allies. The key to this stylistic reinforcement of strategy may be seen in a remark concerning Louis Lomax, a black leader who appeared with Malcolm, and who differed with him. Malcolm used the word "reciprocal," and announced: "That's one of Brother Lomax's words, I stole it from him." Then Malcolm said, "I don't usually deal with big words because I don't usually deal with big people. I deal with small people." Malcolm stated plainly what was clear from his speech—he perceived his audience as the poor, ordinary blacks, his message and style were a direct reflection of this perception. Both the remark and the style it suggests strengthened Malcolm's ethos with those blacks who were beginning to feel alienated from the more affluent middle-class black leadership.

Malcolm's simple and direct language balanced the leadership,

which had been "dillydallying and pussyfooting and compromising,"
while preaching "that 'turn the other cheek' stuff," against most
blacks who daily "catch hell." The use of such a parallel construction put compromise on the same level as footdragging; the language
choice and construction, accordingly, served to help create for his
audience a choice between only two alternatives: Malcolm's black
nationalism or the traditional civil rights approach. The traditional
approach was further rendered unacceptable as Malcolm chose
language to describe and characterize whites. Clearly it was the white
man, Malcolm submitted, who had been "oppressing, exploiting, and
degrading" blacks. There can be no question that Malcolm's style
reflects his conception that *all* white men are on the other side.
Again antithesis served this end as when Malcolm maintained that a
white man "may be friendly, but he's not your friend." "This old,
tricky, blue-eyed liberal who is supposed to be your and my friend,"
is obviously not to be trusted. President Johnson is an "old cracker,"
no better than Eastland of Mississippi; Billy Graham is a white
nationalist; "Hunkies," "Polacks," "Italian refugees," are part of the
American establishment because they are white; the federal power
structure is white and cannot be expected to save black men from
the local authorities because "it's like running from the wolf to the
fox. They're all in cahoots together." The wolf-fox simile, the choice
of adjectives, the comparisons, which language reinforce, are all
designed to promote the conviction that blacks are being "conned."
And the "big Negroes" who cooperate contribute to the subterfuge:
"That's camouflage, that's trickery, that's treachery, window-
dressing." While Roy Wilkins might urge participation in government
through "honorable and competent elected and appointed public
officials," Malcolm saw black rights being stolen and subverted by
"white political crooks." Such a polar situation—white vs. black—
most established black leaders were loath to create, yet Malcolm's
style tended to stress just such a polarity. Even the manner in which
he chose to deny that he was antiwhite underlines this division:". . .
but it does mean we're anti-exploitation, we're anti-degradation,
we're anti-oppression. And if the white man doesn't want us to be
anti-him, let him stop oppressing and exploiting and degrading us."

    To face white hostility and "government conspiracy," Malcolm X
argued that black unity was imperative. It is clear that throughout
the speech the "big words, big people" reference, and the simple,
vernacular language, which supported the image of Malcolm as one

of the black masses,[1] shed light on Malcolm's appeal to the black audience. Again, constructions that presented contrasts were used. The idea that unity could be achieved better through black nationalism, for example, than through the usual civil rights approach was stated: "So it's not necessary to change the white man's mind. We have to change our own mind. You can't change his mind about us. We've got to change our minds about each other."

Malcolm X's speech was a call for black nationalism. Such a cause demanded black unity and a clear, uncompromising view of black oppression. The choice was seen quite literally as a black or white one. It is evident that Malcolm's style reinforced this two-valued conception of the struggle. Such an observation, of course, has far-reaching implications for the critic. Most whites, liberal and conservative, would argue that *all* whites are not alike, that Hubert Humphrey and James Eastland and George Wallace and John Lindsay do not stand in the same position or in the same relationship to black aspirations. Undoubtedly, the stylistic choices that have been discussed briefly, and which could be explored in much greater depth through an examination of the speech text, tend to demonstrate that a polar strategy that blurred differences and avoided subtle distinctions was in operation. This certainly served the purposes of the speaker and may have been the most realistic course to pursue in order to galvanize black efforts and promote black self-consciousness. Arthur L. Smith has argued that "By asking the black community to find its salvation within itself, the black revolutionist gives a sense of independence that was never produced, nor could ever be produced by white rhetoric regardless of how liberal that rhetoric appeared to be."[2] There can be little doubt that the style of Malcolm X was one tactical manifestation of this strategy and was consistent with his perception of the sociological and rhetorical context. Given this perception of the context, Malcolm's style must be recognized as particularly apt.

---

[1] Malcolm's ghetto background, his experiences with crime and in jail, clearly established him as one of the black masses and set him apart from the traditional black middle-class leadership. See *Autobiography of Malcolm X*, New York: Grove, 1965.

[2] Arthur L. Smith, *Rhetoric of Black Revolution*, Boston: Allyn and Bacon, 1969, p. 10. This excellent book offers a careful and penetrating analysis of critical aspects of contemporary black rhetoric.

By 1969, many felt that racial divisions in America had deepened; it was obvious, at least, that serious racial problems had not been solved. In New York City, the liberal Republican Mayor, John Lindsay, was defeated in the primary by a conservative opponent and the Democratic liberals split their primary votes insuring the nomination of a "law and order" conservative. John Lindsay, with the endorsement of New York's Liberal Party and aided by Democratic defections, mounted a campaign against the nominees of the two major parties. Drives for various changes and reforms in America often intersected as black leaders such as Martin Luther King, for example, argued that the war in Vietnam drained off precious resources that could best be devoted to improving the quality of life at home. Some political leaders, notably the mayor of America's largest city, echoed the position. The question became one of priorities: How best could our energies and our money be used to bring our ideals more closely into line with our practices? For those who thought that priorities were cruelly distorted, the question of the best strategy to modify policy was also a critical consideration.

As a protest against the war, a Vietnam Moratorium Day was organized on October 15, 1971. At rallies held throughout New York City, many on college campuses, Mayor Lindsay appeared and delivered the address that follows. The situation compelled the mayor to take into account the recurrent attacks on the antiwar movement as unpatriotic, to emphasize the positive aspects of protest, and to relate the war to the serious urban problems that were the focus of mayorality campaign.

To meet these needs, Lindsay relied heavily on stylistic devices. The short speech contains very little specific evidence to support the Mayor's position. Instead, emotive words are juxtaposed and combined to reinforce the speaker's goals, and abstract words are used to suggest arguments which are not explicitly developed. A brief examination of each of the goals which the constraints of the situation forced upon the mayor will indicate the critical function of style in this speech.

Proponents of the war had called the patriotism of protesters into serious question. Lindsay, in countering this attack, chose words that suggested strong positive values to describe dissent and words of negative value to pose them against. Those who opposed the war were "brave enough, strong enough," to do so. Strength and bravery, qualities not associated with the unpatriotic, were pitted against a "mistaken course." The legitimacy of dissent within the American tradition was a common line of argument developed by peace activists, and Lindsay, too, voiced this contention. He asserted that Americans had "returned to their strongest heritage." The right to free speech, a cardinal principle of American democracy, is a part of the American tradition. Lindsay juxtaposed the city's defense of that right with Washington's denial: After stating that "no man can be denied the right to speak his mind," the mayor pointed out, "This city respects the rights of our public employees, and it will neither punish nor reprimand any man in any office who expresses his own beliefs." And then the contrast: "But neither can we rest content with the charge from Washington that peaceful protest is unpatriotic." The city did not deny rights, Washington, on the other hand, charged those who speak their minds as unpatriotic—the national government's attempt to subvert free speech, to suppress this basic right, was clearly implied through such a construction and contrast. Reiteratimg this theme, Lindsay described the rally as an attempt to "speak out in the great tradition of our history," and charged that the national Administration did "not understand that our greatness comes from the right to speak out—and from the willingness to exercise that right."

Lindsay made use of two other concepts with strong appeal throughout his speech to show the positive nature of the protest and to link the antiwar movement with the city's problems. Again, he did not support these arguments in detail, but relied on the connotative effects of language. "Life" and "reality" are the linguistic tokens that Lindsay used to suggest the positive nature of the protest and to contrast it with government policy. The war had brought "40,000 of our sons and brothers dead . . . destruction and bloodshed . . . a government [in South Vietnam] committed only to its own power and profit." It had left the American people, "divided, tormented, angered, and bewildered." From the "dangerous, self-defeating" course, Lindsay argued, the protest movement hoped to turn the country "again on the work of life." It was an attempt to "save the lives of half a million young Americans," to promote the "nurturing of a better life for us here at home," to "protect the lives of our sons and brothers," to "turn our time away from death, back to the business of life." The oft-repeated plea for life against death is one of the most striking aspects of the style of this speech.

"The business of life," Lindsay further equated with "reality."

The direct references to urban problems in the speech are few. But the call for a realistic policy strongly implied the need to attend to real problems. Early in the speech Mayor Lindsay contrasted the present policy with a peace policy, and he did so in terms of reality: The American people "have said no to illusions and fantasies. They have said yes to reality. They have said yes to peace." The war, which Lindsay labeled "futile and purposeless," was implied to be in direct contradiction to "the business of life." For men who were being wasted in the conflict could better take their place in performing in the task of restoring the cities. "We want them here," Lindsay repeated four times in one short passage. They would be home—"teaching in our schools, cleaning our air and water, making decency and justice facts of life for all of us"—only when "illusions" no longer "survive in Washington."

It would be difficult for any critic to argue that John Lindsay's speech employed a variety of supporting material or brought significant amounts of concrete evidence to bear. The mayor asserted that "What we seek today is not an outburst or emotion. We seek a somber, solemn day of personal inquiry." But it can hardly be denied that his speech relied extensively on language calculated to produce strong emotional reactions and to suggest a wide variety of relationships and associations. This is not to say, however, that such a style made the day less somber or solemn. The fact was that the mayor of New York, immersed in a difficult political campaign, chose to reinforce the attitudes and beliefs of many New Yorkers who dissented from the war. He did not give a speech designed to convert the opposition. Rather he sought to voice the deepest convictions of many of his fellow citizens. That an established political leader, fighting for his political life, chose to do this is in itself worthy of admiration. That he used language so skillfully in this endeavor is worthy of critical approbation.

MALCOLM X

THE BALLOT OR THE BULLET

Mr. Moderator, Brother Lomax, brothers and sisters, friends and enemies, I just can't believe everyone in here is a friend and I don't want to leave anybody out. The question tonight, as I understand it, is "The Negro Revolt, and Where Do We Go From Here?" or "What Next?" In my little humble way of understanding it, it points toward either the ballot or the bullet.

Before we try and explain what is meant by the ballot or the bullet, I would like to clarify something concerning myself. I'm still a Muslim, my religion is still Islam. That's my personal belief. Just as Adam Clayton Powell is a Christian minister who heads the Abyssinian Baptist Church in New York, but at the same time takes part in the political struggles to try and bring about rights to the black people in this country; and Dr. Martin Luther King is a Christian minister down in Atlanta, Georgia, who heads another organization fighting for the civil rights of black people in this country; and Rev. Galamison, I guess you've heard of him, is another Christian minister in New York who has been deeply involved in the school boycotts to eliminate segregated education; well, I myself am a minister, not a Christian minister, but a Muslim minister; and I believe in action on all fronts by whatever means necessary.

Although I'm still a Muslim, I'm not here tonight to discuss my religion. I'm not here to try and change your religion. I'm not here to argue or discuss anything that we differ about, because it's time for us to submerge our differences and realize that it is best for us to first see that we have the same problem, a common problem—a problem that will make you catch hell whether you're a Baptist, or a Methodist, or a Muslim, or a nationalist. Whether you're educated or illiterate, whether you live on the boulevard or in the alley, you're going to catch hell just like I am. We're all in the same boat and we all are going to catch the same hell from the same man. He just happens to be a white man. All of us have suffered here, in this country, political oppression at the hands of the white man,

Malcolm X's speech was given in Cleveland on April 3, 1964. It is reprinted by permission of Pathfinder Press from George Brietman, ed., *Malcolm X Speaks*, copyright 1965 by Betty Shabazz and Merit Publishers.

economic exploitation at the hands of the white man, and social
degradation at the hands of the white man.

Now in speaking like this, it doesn't mean that we're anti-white,
but it does mean we're anti-exploitation, we're anti-degradation,
we're anti-oppression. And if the white man doesn't want us to be
anti-him, let him stop oppressing and exploiting and degrading us.
Whether we are Christians or Muslims or nationalists or agnostics or
atheists, we must first learn to forget our differences. If we have
differences, let us differ in the closet; when we come out in front, let
us not have anything to argue about until we get finished arguing
with the man. If the late President Kennedy could get together with
Khrushchev and exchange some wheat, we certainly have more in
common with each other than Kennedy and Khrushchev had with
each other.

If we don't do something real soon, I think you'll have to agree
that we're going to be forced either to use the ballot or the bullet.
It's one or the other in 1964. It isn't that time is running out—time
has run out! 1964 threatens to be the most explosive year America
has ever witnessed. The most explosive year. Why? It's also a
political year. It's the year when all of the white political crooks will
be right back in your and my community with their false promises,
building up our hopes for a letdown, with their trickery and their
treachery, with their false promises which they don't intend to keep.
As they nourish these dissatisfactions, it can only lead to one thing,
an explosion; and now we have the type of black man on the scene
in America today—I'm sorry, Brother Lomax—who just doesn't
intend to turn the other cheek any longer.

Don't let anybody tell you anything about the odds are against
you. If they draft you, they send you to Korea and make you face
800 million Chinese. If you can be brave over there, you can be
brave right here. These odds aren't as great as those odds. And if you
fight here, you will at least know what you're fighting for.

I'm not a politician, not even a student of politics; in fact, I'm not
a student of much of anything. I'm not a Democrat, I'm not a
Republican, and I don't even consider myself an American. If you
and I were Americans, there'd be no problem. Those Hunkies that
just got off the boat, they're already Americans; Polacks are already
Americans; the Italian refugees are already Americans. Everything
that came out of Europe, every blue-eyed thing, is already an
American. And as long as you and I have been over here, we aren't
Americans yet.

Well, I am one who doesn't believe in deluding myself. I'm not going to sit at your table and watch you eat, with nothing on my plate, and call myself a diner. Sitting at the table doesn't make you a diner, unless you eat some of what's on that plate. Being here in America doesn't make you an American. Being born here in America doesn't make you an American. Why, if birth made you American, you wouldn't need any legislation, you wouldn't need any amendments to the Constitution, you wouldn't be faced with civil-rights filibustering in Washington, D.C. right now. They don't have to pass civil-rights legislation to make a Polack an American.

No, I'm not an American. I'm one of the 22 million black people who are the victims of Americanism. One of the 22 million black people who are the victims of democracy, nothing but disguised hypocrisy. So, I'm not standing here speaking to you as an American, or a patriot, or a flag-saluter, or a flag-waver—no, not I. I'm speaking as a victim of this American system. And I see America through the eyes of the victim. I don't see any American dream; I see an American nightmare.

These 22 million victims are waking up. Their eyes are coming open. They're beginning to see what they used to only look at. They're becoming politically mature. They are realizing that there are new political trends from coast to coast. As they see these new political trends, it's possible for them to see that every time there's an election the races are so close that they have to have a recount. They had to recount in Massachusetts to see who was going to be governor, it was so close. It was the same way in Rhode Island, in Minnesota, and in many other parts of the country. And the same with Kennedy and Nixon when they ran for president. It was so close they had to count all over again. Well, what does this mean? It means that when white people are evenly divided, and black people have a bloc of votes of their own, it is left up to them to determine who's going to sit in the White House and who's going to be in the dog house.

It was the black man's vote that put the present administration in Washington, D.C. Your vote, your dumb vote, your ignorant vote, your wasted vote put in an administration in Washington, D.C., that has seen fit to pass every kind of legislation imaginable, saving you until last, then filibustering on top of that. And your and my leaders have the audacity to run around clapping their hands and talk about how much progress we're making. And what a good president we have. If he wasn't good in Texas, he sure can't be good in Washing-

ton, D.C. Because Texas is a lynch state, it is in the same breath as
Mississippi, no different; only they lynch you in Texas with a Texas
accent and lynch you in Mississippi with a Mississippi accent. And
these Negro leaders have the audacity to go and have some coffee in
the White House with a Texan, a Southern cracker—that's all he ➤
is—and then come out and tell you and me that he's going to be
better for us because, since he's from the South, he knows how to
deal with the Southerners. What kind of logic is that? Let Eastland
be president, he's from the South too. He should be better able to
deal with them than Johnson.

In this present administration they have in the House of Representatives 257 Democrats to only 177 Republicans. They control
two-thirds of the House vote. Why can't they pass something that
will help you and me? In the Senate, there are 67 senators who are
of the Democratic Party. Only 33 of them are Republicans. Why, the
Democrats have got the government sewed up, and you're the one
who sewed it up for them. And what have they given you for it?
Four years in office, and just now getting around to some civil-rights
legislation. Just now, after everything else is gone, out of the way,
they're going to sit down now and play with you all summer
long—the same old giant con game that they call filibuster. All those
are in cahoots together. Don't you ever think they're not in cahoots
together, for the man that is heading the civil-rights filibuster is a
man from Georgia named Richard Russell. When Johnson became
president, the first man he asked for when he got back to Washington, D.C., was "Dicky"—that's how tight they are. That's his boy,
that's his pal, that's his buddy. But they're playing that old con
game. One of them makes believe he's for you, and he's got it fixed
where the other one is so tight against you, he never has to keep his
promise.

So it's time in 1964 to wake up. And when you see them coming
up with that kind of conspiracy, let them know your eyes are open.
And let them know you got something else that's wide open too. It's
got to be the ballot or the bullet. The ballot or the bullet. If you're
afraid to use an expression like that, you should get on out of the
country, you should get back in the cotton patch, you should get
back in the alley. They get all the Negro vote, and after they get it,
the Negro gets nothing in return. All they did when they got to
Washington was give a few big Negroes big jobs. Those big Negroes
didn't need big jobs, they already had jobs. That's camouflage, that's

trickery, that's treachery, window-dressing. I'm not trying to knock out the Democrats for the Republicans, we'll get to them in a minute. But it is true—you put the Democrats first and the Democrats put you last.

Look at it the way it is. What alibis do they use, since they control Congress and the Senate? What alibi do they use when you and I ask, "Well, when are you going to keep your promise?" They blame the Dixiecrats. What is a Dixiecrat? A Democrat. A Dixiecrat is nothing but a Democrat in disguise. The titular head of the Democrats is also the head of the Dixiecrats, because the Dixiecrats are a part of the Democratic Party. The Democrats have never kicked the Dixiecrats out of the party. The Dixiecrats bolted themselves once, but the Democrats didn't put them out. Imagine, these lowdown Southern segregationists put the Northern Democrats down. But the Northern Democrats have never put the Dixiecrats down. No, look at that thing the way it is. They have got a con game going on, a political con game, and you and I are in the middle. It's time for you and me to wake up and start looking at it like it is, and trying to understand it like it is; and then we can deal with it like it is.

The Dixiecrats in Washington, D.C., control the key committees that run the government. The only reason the Dixiecrats control these committees is because they have seniority. The only reason they have seniority is because they come from states where Negroes can't vote. This is not even a government that's based on democracy. It is not a government that is made up of representatives of the people. Half of the people in the South can't even vote. Eastland is not even supposed to be in Washington. Half of the senators and congressmen who occupy these key positions in Washington, D.C., are there illegally, are there unconstitutionally.

I was in Washington, D.C., a week ago Thursday, when they were debating whether or not they should let the bill come onto the floor. And in the back of the room where the Senate meets, there's a huge map of the United States, and on that map it shows the location of Negroes throughout the country. And it shows that the Southern section of the country, the states that are most heavily concentrated with Negroes, are the ones that have senators and congressmen standing up filibustering and doing all other kinds of trickery to keep the Negro from being able to vote. This is pitiful. But it's not pitiful for us any longer; it's actually pitiful for the white man, because soon now, as the Negro awakens a little more and sees the vise that he's in, sees the bag that he's in, sees the real game that he's in, then the Negro's going to develop a new tactic.

These senators and congressmen actually violate the constitutional amendments that guarantee the people of that particular state or county the right to vote. And the Constitution itself has within it the machinery to expel any representative from a state where the voting rights of the people are violated. You don't even need new legislation. Any person in Congress right now, who is there from a state or a district where the voting rights of the people are violated, that particular person should be expelled from Congress. And when you expel him, you've removed one of the obstacles in the path of any real meaningful legislation in this country. In fact, when you expel them, you don't need new legislation, because they will be replaced by black representatives from counties and districts where the black man is in the majority, not in the minority.

If the black man in these Southern states had his full voting rights, the key Dixiecrats in Washington, D.C., which means the key Democrats in Washington, D.C., would lose their seats. The Democratic Party itself would lose its power. It would cease to be powerful as a party. When you see the amount of power that would be lost by the Democratic Party if it were to lose the Dixiecrat wing, or branch, or element, you can see where it's against the interests of the Democrats to give voting rights to Negroes in States where the Democrats have been in complete power and authority ever since the Civil War. You just can't belong to that party without analyzing it.

I say again, I'm not anti-Democrat, I'm not anti-Republican, I'm not anti-anything. I'm just questioning their sincerity, and some of the strategy that they've been using on our people by promising them promises that they don't intend to keep. When you keep the Democrats in power, you're keeping the Dixiecrats in power. I doubt that my good Brother Lomax will deny that. A vote for a Democrat is a vote for a Dixiecrat. That's why, in 1964, it's time now for you and me to become more politically mature and realize what the ballot is for; what we're supposed to get when we cast a ballot; and that if we don't cast a ballot, it's going to end up in a situation where we're going to have to cast a bullet. It's either a ballot or a bullet.

In the North, they do it a different way. They have a system that's known as gerrymandering, whatever that means. It means when Negroes become too heavily concentrated in a certain area, and begin to gain too much political power, the white man comes along and changes the district lines. You may say, "Why do you keep

saying white man?" Because it's the white man who does it. I
haven't ever seen any Negro changing any lines. They don't let him
get near the line. It's the white man who does this. And usually, it's
the white man who grins at you the most, and pats you on the back,
and is supposed to be your friend. He may be friendly, but he's not
your friend.

So, what I'm trying to impress upon you, in essence, is this: You
and I in America are faced not with a segregationist conspiracy, we're
faced with a government conspiracy. Everyone who's filibustering is
a senator—that's the government. Everyone who's finagling in
Washington, D.C., is a congressman—that's the government. You
don't have anybody putting blocks in your path but people who are
a part of the government. The same government that you go abroad
to fight for and die for is the government that is in conspiracy to
deprive you of your voting rights, deprive you of your economic
opportunities, deprive you of decent housing, deprive you of decent
education. You don't need to go to the employer alone, it is the
government itself, the government of America, that is responsible for
the oppression and exploitation and degradation of black people in
this country. And you should drop it in their lap. This government
has failed the Negro. This so-called democracy has failed the Negro.
And all these white liberals have definitely failed the Negro.

So, where do we go from here? First, we need some friends. We
need some new allies. The entire civil-rights struggle needs a new
interpretation, a broader interpretation. We need to look at this
civil-rights thing from another angle—from the inside as well as from
the outside. To those of us whose philosophy is black nationalism,
the only way you can get involved in the civil-rights struggle is give it
a new interpretation. That old interpretation excluded us. It kept us
out. So, we're giving a new interpretation to the civil-rights struggle,
an interpretation that will enable us to come into it, take part in it.
And these handkerchief-heads who have been dillydallying and
pussyfooting and compromising—we don't intend to let them
pussyfoot and dillydally and compromise any longer.

How can you thank a man for giving you what's already yours?
How then can you thank him for giving you only part of what's
already yours? You haven't even made progress, if what's being given
to you, you should have had already. That's not progress. And I love
my Brother Lomax, the way he pointed out we're right back where
we were in 1954. We're not even as far up as we were in 1954. We're
behind where we were in 1954. There's more segregation now than
there was in 1954. There's more racial animosity, more racial hatred,

more racial violence today in 1964, than there was in 1954. Where is
the progress?

And now you're facing a situation where the young Negro's
coming up. They don't want to hear that "turn-the-other cheek"
stuff, no. In Jacksonville, those were teen-agers, they were throwing
Molotov cocktails. Negroes have never done that before. But it
shows you there's a new deal coming in. There's new thinking
coming in. There's new strategy coming in. It'll be Molotov cocktails
this month, hand grenades next month, and something else next
month. It'll be ballots, or it'll be bullets. It'll be liberty, or it will be
death. The only difference about this kind of death—it'll be
reciprocal. You know what is meant by "reciprocal"? That's one of
Brother Lomax's words, I stole it from him. I don't usually deal with
those big words because I don't usually deal with big people. I deal
with small people. I find you can get a whole lot of small people and
whip hell out of a whole lot of big people. They haven't got
anything to lose, and they've got everything to gain. And they'll let
you know in a minute: "It takes two to tango; when I go, you go."

The black nationalists, those whose philosophy is black nationalism, in bringing about this new interpretation of the entire
meaning of civil rights, look upon it as meaning, as Brother Lomax
has pointed out, equality of opportunity. Well, we're justified in
seeking civil rights, if it means equality of opportunity, because all
we're doing there is trying to collect for our investment. Our
mothers and fathers invested sweat and blood. Three hundred and
ten years we worked in this country without a dime in return—I
mean with a *dime* in return. You let the white man walk around here
talking about how rich this country is, but you never stop to think
how it got rich so quick. It got rich because you made it rich.

You take the people who are in this audience right now. They're
poor, we're all poor as individuals. Our weekly salary individually
amounts to hardly anything. But if you take the salary of everyone
in here collectively it'll fill up a whole lot of baskets. It's a lot of
wealth. If you can collect the wages of just these people right here
for a year, you'll be rich—richer than rich. When you look at it like
that, think how rich Uncle Sam had to become, not with this
handful, but millions of black people. Your and my mother and
father, who didn't work an eight-hour shift, but worked from "can't
see" in the morning until "can't see" at night, and worked for
nothing, making the white man rich, making Uncle Sam rich.

This is our investment. This is our contribution—our blood. Not

only did we give of our free labor, we gave of our blood. Every time
he had a call to arms, we were the first ones in uniform. We died on
every battlefield the white man had. We have made a greater sacrifice
than anybody who's standing up in America today. We have made a
greater contribution and have collected less. Civil rights, for those of
us whose philosophy is black nationalism, means: "Give it to us
now. Don't wait for next year. Give it to us yesterday, and that's not
fast enough."

I might stop right here to point out one thing. Whenever you're
going after something that belongs to you, anyone who's depriving
you of the right to have it is a criminal. Understand that. Whenever
you are going after something that is yours, you are within your
legal rights to lay claim to it. And anyone who puts forth any effort
to deprive you of that which is yours, is breaking the law, is a
criminal. And this was pointed out by the Supreme Court decision.
It outlawed segregation. Which means segregation is against the law.
Which means a segregationist is breaking the law. A segregationist is
a criminal. You can't label him as anything other than that. And
when you demonstrate against segregation, the law is on your side.
The Supreme Court is on your side.

Now, who is it that opposes you in carrying out the law; The
police department itself. With police dogs and clubs. Whenever you
demonstrate against segregation, whether it is segregated education,
segregated housing, or anything else, the law is on your side, and
anyone who stands in the way is not the law any longer. They are
breaking the law, they are not representatives of the law. Any time
you demonstrate against segregation and a man has the audacity to
put a police dog on you, kill that dog, kill him, I'm telling you, kill
that dog. I say it, if they put me in jail tomorrow, kill—that—dog.
Then you'll put a stop to it. Now, if these white people in here don't
want to see that kind of action, get down and tell the mayor to tell
the police department to pull the dogs in. That's all you have to do.
If you don't do it, someone else will.

If you don't take this kind of stand, your little children will grow
up and look at you and think "shame." If you don't take an
uncompromising stand—I don't mean go out and get violent; but at
the same time you should never be nonviolent unless you run into
some nonviolence. I'm nonviolent with those who are nonviolent
with me. But when you drop that violence on me, then you've made
me go insane, and I'm not responsible for what I do. And that's the
way every Negro should get. Any time you know you're within the

law, within your legal rights, within your moral rights, in accord
with justice, then die for what you believe in. But don't die alone.
Let your dying be reciprocal. This is what is meant by equality.
What's good for the goose is good for the gander.

When we begin to get in this area, we need new friends, we need
new allies. We need to expand the civil-rights struggle to a higher
level—to the level of human rights. Whenever you are in a civil-rights
struggle, whether you know it or not, you are confining yourself to
the jurisdiction of Uncle Sam. No one from the outside world can
speak out in your behalf as long as your struggle is a civil-rights
struggle. Civil rights comes within the domestic affairs of this
country. All of our African brothers and our Asian brothers and our
Latin-American brothers cannot open their mouths and interfere in
the domestic affairs of the United States. And as long as it's civil
rights, this comes under the jurisdiction of Uncle Sam.

But the United Nations has what's known as the charter of human
rights, it has a committee that deals in human rights. You may
wonder why all of the atrocities that have been committed in Africa
and in Hungary and in Asia and in Latin America are brought before
the UN, and the Negro problem is never brought before the UN. This
is part of the conspiracy. This old, tricky, blue-eyed liberal who is
supposed to be your and my friend, supposed to be in our corner,
supposed to be subsidizing our struggle, and supposed to be acting in
the capacity of an adviser, never tells you anything about human
rights. They keep you wrapped up in civil rights. And you spend so
much time barking up the civil-rights tree, you don't even know
there's a human-rights tree on the same floor.

When you expand the civil-rights struggle to the level of human
rights, you can then take the case of the black man in this country
before the nations in the UN. You can take it before the General
Assembly. You can take Uncle Sam before a world court. But the
only level you can do it on is the level of human rights. Civil rights
keeps you under his restrictions, under his jurisdiction. Civil rights
keeps you in his pocket. Civil rights means you're asking Uncle Sam
to treat you right. Human rights are something you were born with.
Human rights are your God-given rights, you can take them to the
world court. Uncle Sam's hands are dripping with blood, dripping
with the blood of the black man in this country. He's the earth's
number-one hypocrite. He has the audacity—yes, he has—imagine
him posing as the leader of the free world. The free world!—and you
over here singing "We Shall Overcome." Expand the civil-rights

struggle to the level of human rights, take it into the United Nations, where our African brothers can throw their weight on our side, where our Asian brothers can throw their weight on our side, where our Latin-American brothers can throw their weight on our side, and where 800 million Chinamen are sitting there waiting to throw their weight on our side.

Let the world know how bloody his hands are. Let the world know the hypocrisy that's practiced over here. Let it be the ballot or the bullet. Let him know that it must be the ballot or the bullet.

When you take your case to Washington, D.C., you're taking it to the criminal who's responsible; it's like running from the wolf to the fox. They're all in cahoots together. They all work political chicanery and make you look like a chump before the eyes of the world. Here you are walking around in America, getting ready to be drafted and sent abroad, like a tin soldier, and when you get over there, people ask you what are you fighting for, and you have to stick your tongue in your cheek. No, take Uncle Sam to court, take him before the world.

By ballot I only mean freedom. Don't you know—I disagree with Lomax on this issue—that the ballot is more important than the dollar? Can I prove it? Yes. Look in the UN. There are poor nations in the UN; yet those poor nations can get together with their voting power and keep the rich nations from making a move. They have one nation—one vote, everyone has an equal vote. And when those brothers from Asia, and Africa and the darker parts of this earth get together, their voting power is sufficient to hold Sam in check. Or Russia in check. Or some other section of the earth in check. So, the ballot is most important.

Right now, in this country, if you and I, 22 million African-Americans—that's what we are Africans who are in America. You're nothing but Africans. Nothing but Africans. In fact, you'd get farther calling yourself African instead of Negro. Africans don't catch hell. You're the only one catching hell. They don't have to pass civil-rights bills for Africans. An African can go anywhere he wants right now. All you've got to do is tie your head up. That's right, go anywhere you want. Just stop being a Negro. Change your name to Hoogagagooba. That'll show you how silly the white man is. You're dealing with a silly man. A friend of mine who's very dark put a turban on his head and went into a restaurant in Atlanta before they called themselves desegregated. He went into a white restaurant, he sat down, they served him, and he said, "What would

happen if a Negro came in here?" And there he's sitting, black as
night, but because he had his head wrapped up the waitress looked
back at him and says, "Why, there wouldn't no nigger dare come in
here."

So, you're dealing with a man whose bias and prejudice are
making him lose his mind, his intelligence, every day. He's frightened. He looks around and sees what's taking place on this earth,
and he sees that the pendulum of time is swinging in your direction.
The dark people are waking up. They're losing their fear of the white
man. No place where he's fighting right now is he winning.
Everywhere he's fighting, he's fighting someone your and my
complexion. And they're beating him. He can't win any more. He's
won his last battle. He failed to win the Korean War. He couldn't
win it. He had to sign a truce. That's a loss. Any time Uncle Sam,
with all his machinery for warfare, is held to draw by some
rice-eaters, he's lost the battle. He had to sign a truce. America's not
supposed to sign a truce. She's supposed to be bad. But she's not bad
any more. She's bad as long as she can use her hydrogen bomb, but
she can't use hers for fear Russia might use hers. Russia can't use
hers, for fear Sam might use his. So, both of them are weaponless.
They can't use the weapon because each's weapon nullifies the
other's. So the only place where action can tak place is on the
ground. And the white man can't win another war fighting on the
ground. Those days are over. The black man knows it, the brown
man knows it, the red man knows it, and the yellow man knows it.
So they engage him in guerrilla warfare. That's not his style. You've
got to have heart to be a guerrilla warrior, and he hasn't got any
heart. I'm telling you now.

I just want to give you a little briefing on guerrilla warfare
because, before you know it, before you know it—it takes heart to
be a guerrilla warrior because you're on your own. In conventional
warfare you have tanks and a whole lot of other people with you to
back you up, planes over your head and all that kind of stuff. But a
guerrilla is on his own. All you have is a rifle, some sneakers and a
bowl of rice, and that's all you need—and a lot of heart. The
Japanese on some of those islands in the Pacific, when the American
soldiers landed, one Japanese sometimes could hold the whole army
off. He'd just wait until the sun went down, and when the sun went
down they were all equal. He would take his little blade and slip
from bush to bush, and from American to American. The white

soldiers couldn't cope with that. Whenever you see a white soldier
that fought in the Pacific, he has the shakes, he has a nervous
condition, because they scared him to death.

The same thing happened to the French up in French Indochina.
People who just a few years previously were rice farmers got
together and ran the the heavily-mechanized French army out of
Indochina. You don't need it—modern warfare today won't work.
This is the day of the guerrilla. They did the same thing in Algeria.
Algerians, who were nothing but Bedouins, took a rifle and sneaked
off to the hills, and de Gaulle and all of his high-falutin' war
machinery couldn't defeat those guerrillas. Nowhere on this earth
does the white man win in a guerrilla warfare. It's not his speed. Just
as guerrilla warfare is prevailing in Asia and in parts of Africa and in
parts of Latin America, you've got to be mighty naive, or you've got
to play the black man cheap, if you don't think some day he's going
to wake up and find that it's got to be the ballot or the bullet.

I would like to say, in closing, a few things concerning the Muslim
Mosque, Inc., which we established recently in New York City. It's
true we're Muslims and our religion is Islam, but we don't mix our
religion with our politics and our economics and our social and civil
activities—not any more. We keep our religion in our mosque. After
our religious services are over, then as Muslims we become involved
in political action, economic action and social and civic action. We
become involved with anybody, anywhere, any time and in any
manner that's designed to eliminate the evils, the political, economic
and social evils that are afflicting the people of our community.

The political philosophy of black nationalism means that the
black man should control the politics and the politicians in his own
community; no more. The black man in the black community has to
be re-educated into the science of politics so he will know what
politics is supposed to bring him in return. Don't be throwing out
any ballots. A ballot is like a bullet. You don't throw your ballots
until you see a target, and if that target is not within your reach,
keep your ballot in your pocket. The political philosophy of black
nationalism is being taught in the Christian church. It's being taught
in the NAACP. It's being taught in CORE meetings. It's being taught
in SNCC (Student Nonviolent Coordinating Committee) meetings.
It's being taught in Muslim meetings. It's being taught where nothing
but atheists and agnostics come together. It's being taught every-

where. Black people are fed up with the dillydallying, pussyfooting, compromising approach that we've been using toward getting our freedom. We want freedom now, but we're not going to get it saying "We Shall Overcome." We've got to fight until we overcome.

The economic philosophy of black nationalism is pure and simple. It only means that we should control the economy of our community. Why should white people be running all the stores in our community? Why should white people be running the banks of our community ? Why should the economy of our community be in the hands of the white man? Why? If a black man can't move his store into a white community, you tell me why a white man should move his store into a black community. The philsophy of black nationalism involves a re-education program in the black community in regards to economics. Our people have to be made to see that any time you take your dollar out of your community and spend it in a community where you don't live, the community where you live will get poorer and poorer, and the community where you spend your money will get richer and richer. Then you wonder why where you live is always a ghetto or a slum area. And where you and I are concerned, not only do we lose it when we spend it out of the community, but the white man has got all our stores in the community tied up; so that though we spend it in the community, at sundown the man who runs the store takes it over across town somewhere. He's got us in a vise.

So the economic philosophy of black nationalism means in every church, in every civic organization, in every fraternal order, it's time now for our people to become conscious of the importance of controlling the economy of our community. If we own the stores, if we operate the businesses, if we try and establish some industry in our own community, then we're developing to the position where we are creating employment for our own kind. Once you gain control of the economy of your own community, then you don't have to picket and boycott and beg some cracker downtown for a job in his business.

The social philosophy of black nationalism only means that we have to get together and remove the evils, the vices, alcoholism, drug addiction, and other evils that are destroying the moral fiber of our community. We ourselves have to lift the level of our community, the standard of our community to a higher level, make our own society beautiful so that we will be satisfied in our own social circles and won't be running around here trying to knock our way into a social circle where we're not wanted.

So I say, in spreading a gospel such as black nationalism, it is not designed to make the black man re-evaluate the white man—you know him already—but to make the black man re-evaluate himself. Don't change the white man's mind—you can't change his mind, and that whole thing about appealing to the moral conscience of America—America's conscience is bankrupt. She lost all conscience a long time ago. Uncle Sam has no conscience. They don't know what morals are. They don't try and eliminate an evil because it's evil, or because it's illegal, or because it's immoral; they eliminate it only when it threatens their existence. So you're wasting your time appealing to the moral conscience of a bankrupt man like Uncle Sam. If he had a conscience, he'd straighten this thing out with no more pressure being put upon him. So it is not necessary to change the white man's mind. We have to change our own mind. You can't change his mind about us. We've got to change our own minds about each other. We have to see each other with new eyes. We have to see each other as brothers and sisters. We have to come together with warmth so we can develop unity and harmony that's necessary to get this problem solved ourselves. How can we do this? How can we avoid jealousy? How can we avoid the suspicion and the divisions that exist in the community. I'll tell you how.

I have watched how Billy Graham comes into a city, spreading what he calls the gospel of Christ, which is only white nationalism. That's what he is. Billy Graham is a white nationalist; I'm a black nationalist. But since it's the natural tendency for leaders to be jealous and look upon a powerful figure like Graham with suspicion and envy, how is it possible for him to come into a city and get all the cooperation of the church leaders? Don't think because they're church leaders that they don't have weaknesses that make them envious and jealous—no, everybody's got it. It's not an accident that when they want to choose a cardinal (as Pope) over there in Rome, they get in a closet so you can't hear them cussing and fighting and carrying on.

Billy Graham comes in preaching the gospel of Christ, he evangelizes the gospel, he stirs everybody up, but he never tries to start a church. If he came in trying to start a church, all the churches would be against him. So, he just comes in talking about Christ and tells everybody who gets Christ to go to any church where Christ is; and in this way the church co-operates with him. So we're going to take a page from his book.

Our Gospel is black nationalism. We're not trying to threaten the existence of any organization, but we're spreading the gospel of black nationalism. Anywhere there's a church that is also preaching and practicing the gospel of black nationalism, join that church. If the NAACP is preaching and practicing the gospel of black nationalism, join the NAACP. If CORE is spreading and practicing the gospel of black nationlaism, join CORE. Join any organization that has a gospel that's for the uplift of the black man. And when you get into it and see them pussyfooting or compromising, pull out of it because that's not black nationalism. We'll find another one.

And in this manner, the organizations will increase in number and in quantity and in quality, and by August, it is then our intention to have a black nationalist convention which will consist of delegates from all over the country who are interested in the political, economic and social philosophy of black nationalism. After these delegates convene, we will hold a seminar, we will hold discussions, we will listen to everyone. We want to hear new ideas and new solutions and new answers. And at that time, if we see fit then to form a black nationalist party, we'll form a black nationalist party. If it's necessary to form a black nationalist army, we'll form a black nationalist army. It'll be the ballot or the bullet. It'll be liberty or it'll be death.

It's time for you and me to stop sitting in this country, letting some cracker senators, Northern crackers and Southern crackers, sit there in Washington, D.C., and come to a conclusion in their mind that you and I are supposed to have civil rights. There's no white man going to tell me anything about my rights. Brothers and sisters, always remember, if it doesn't take senators and congressmen and presidential proclamations to give freedom to the white man, it is not necessary for legislation or proclamation or Supreme Court decisions to give freedom to the black man. You let that white man know, if this is a country of freedom, let it be a country of freedom; and if it's not a country of freedom, change it.

We will work with anybody, anywhere at any time, who is genuinely interested in tackling the problem head-on, nonviolently as long as the enemy is nonviolent, but violent when the enemy gets violent. We'll work with you on the voter-registration drive, we'll work with you on rent strikes, we'll work with you on school boycotts—I don't believe in any kind of integration; I'm not even worried about it because I know you're not going to get it anyway; you're not going to get it because you're afraid to die; you've got to be ready to die if you try and force yourself on the white man, because he'll get just as violent as those crackers in Mississippi, right

here in Cleveland. But we will still work with you on the school
boycotts because we're against a segregated school system. A
segregated school system produces children who, when they
graduate, graduate with crippled minds. But this does not mean that
a school is segregated because it's all black. A segregated school
means a school that is controlled by people who have no real interest
in it whatsoever.

Let me explain what I mean. A segregated district or community
is a community in which people live, but outsiders control the
politics and the economy of that community. They never refer to
the white section as a segregated community. Why? The white man
controls his own school, his own bank, his own economy, his own
politics, his own everything, his own community—but he also
controls yours. When you're under someone else's control, you're
segregated. They'll always give you the lowest or the worst that
there is to offer, but it doesn't mean you're segregated just because
you have your own. You've got to control your own. Just like the
white man has control of his, you need to control yours.

You know the best way to get rid of segregation? The white man
is more afraid of separation than he is of integration. Segregation
means that he puts you away from him, but not far enough for you
to be out of his jurisdiction; separation means you're gone. And the
white man will integrate faster than he'll let you separate. So we will
work with you against the segregated school system because it's
criminal, because it is absolutely destructive, in every way imaginable, to the minds of the children who have to be exposed to that
type of crippling education.

Last but not least, I must say this concerning the great controversy over rifles and shotguns. The only thing that I've ever said is
that in areas where the government has proven itself either unwilling
or unable to defend the lives and the property of Negroes, it's time
for Negroes to defend themselves. Article number two of the
constitutional amendments provides you and me the right to own a
rifle or a shotgun. It is constitutionally legal to own a shotgun or a
rifle. This doesn't mean you're going to get a rifle and form
battalions and go out looking for white folks, although you'd be
within your rights—I mean, you'd be justified; but that would be
illegal and we don't do anything illegal. If the white man doesn't
want the black man buying rifles and shotguns, then let the
government do its job. That's all. And don't let the white man come
to you and ask you what you think about what Malcolm says—why,

you old Uncle Tom. He would never ask you if he thought you were going to say, "Amen!" No, he is making a Tom out of you.

So, this doesn't mean forming rifle clubs and going out looking for people, but it is time, in 1964, if you are a man, to let that man know. If he's not going to do his job in running the government and providing you and me with the protection that our taxes are supposed to be for, since he spends all those billions for his defense budget, he certainly can't begrudge you and me spending $12 or $15 for a single-shot, or double-action. I hope you understand. Don't go out shooting people, but any time, brothers and sisters, and especially the men in the audience some of you wearing Congressional Medals of Honor, with shoulders this wide, chests this big, muscles that big—any time you and I sit around and read where they bomb a church and murder in cold blood, not some grownups, but four little girls while they were praying to the same god the white man taught them to pray to, and you and I see the government go down and can't find who did it.

Why, this man—he can find Eichmann hiding down in Argentina somewhere. Let two or three American soldiers, who are minding somebody else's business way over in South Vietnam, get killed, and he'll send battleships, sticking his nose in their business. He wanted to send troops down to Cuba and make them have what he calls free elections—this old cracker who doesn't have free elections in his own country. No, if you never see me another time in your life, if I die in the morning, I'll die saying one thing: the ballot or the bullet, the ballot or the bullet.

If a Negro in 1964 has to sit around and wait for some cracker senator to filibuster when it comes to the rights of black people, why, you and I should hang our heads in shame. You talk about a march on Washington in 1963, you haven't seen anything. There's some more going down in '64. And this time they're not going like they went last year. They're not going singing "We Shall Overcome." They're not going with white friends. They're not going with placards already painted for them. They're not going with round-trip tickets. They're going with one-way tickets.

And if they don't want that non-nonviolent army going down there, tell them to bring the filibuster to a halt. The black nationalists aren't going to wait. Lyndon B. Johnson is the head of the Democratic Party. If he's for civil rights, let him go into the Senate next week and declare himself. Let him go in there right now and declare himself. Let him go in there and denounce the Southern branch of his party. Let him go in there right now and take a moral stand—right now, not later. Tell him, don't wait until election time. If he waits too long, brothers and sisters, he will be responsible for letting a condition develop in this country which will create a climate that will bring seeds up out of the ground with vegetation on the end of them looking like something these people never dreamed of. In 1964, it's the ballot or the bullet. Thank you.

JOHN V. LINDSAY

VIETNAM MORATORIUM ADDRESS

"We learn from history," a cynic once said, "that men learn nothing from history."

We are here today because we have learned from history. We have learned that the war in Vietnam has divided two nations. We have learned that it has brought us neither a sense of victory nor a sense of pride. We have learned that the American people are brave enough, strong enough to change a mistaken course. And we have learned that the time has at long last come for this war to stop.

America has looked into the face of war for five years. We have found 40,000 of our sons and brothers dead. We have found untold destruction and bloodshed in Vietnam. We have found a government committed only to its own power and profit. And we have found us a people divided, tormented, angered and bewildered.

Now, at long last, the people of America have returned to their strongest heritage—the heritage of independent judgment. And they have said no to illusions and fantasies. They have said yes to reality. They have said yes to peace.

This gathering is a part of that affirmation. It is part of an effort—all over New York, all over America—to convey a sense of personal concern by all of us. What we seek today is not outburst or emotion. We seek a somber, solemn day of personal inquiry.

We seek, first of all, to ask every citizen to examine his own conscience—and to share this concern with his neighbor. We do not

John V. Lindsay's speech was given in New York City on October 15, 1969. It is reprinted by permission of Thomas B. Morgan.

ask conformity. We ask those who still support this war to speak
their minds, to discuss this war with their neighbors and workers. We
ask those who oppose this war not to talk among ourselves—but to
engage in discussion in the neighborhoods of this city.

For no man can be denied the right to speak his mind. This city
respects the rights of our public employees, and it will neither
punish nor reprimand any man in any office who expresses his own
beliefs.

But neither can we rest content with the charge from Washington
that this peaceful protest is unpatriotic. We heard that charge five
years ago. We heard it three years ago. Tragically, new voices are
speaking the same sounds again.

But the fact is that this dissent is the highest form of patriotism. It
is an attempt to turn this nation away from a dangerous, self-
defecting course, and to set us again on the work of life.

It is an attempt to save the lives of a half million young Americans—by extricating them from this futile and purposeless war.

It is an attempt to turn the massive resources of this Nation to
work not in destruction—but in the nurturing of a better life for us
here at home.

And it is an attempt, above all, to speak out in the great tradition
of our history—not through violence and discord, but through
peaceful debate and solemn witness. Those who charge that this is
unpatriotic do not know the history of their own Nation. And they
do not understand that our greatness comes from the right to speak
out—and from the willingness to exercise that right.

So we meet today: To mourn our honored dead. To end the war
in Vietnam. To protect the lives of our sons and brothers by bringing
them home.

For we want them here: To work and to marry. We want them
here—to raise their children and live out their lives in peace. We want
them here—to join in binding up our Nation's wounds. And we want
them here—teaching in our schools, cleaning our air and water,
making decency and justice facts of life for all of us.

And to this goal we dedicate ourselves: Today and in the days and
weeks beyond. We pledge to say no to this war, and to say yes to
peace, and to the lives of our fighting men—whom we honor today
for their courage in this most tragic conflict. We say yes to the work
of stopping this war.

We cannot know how long it will take. We cannot know how long
illusions will survive in Washington. But we know what we must

do—today and in the days beyond. And that is to speak out—among our friends and colleagues—until this Nation ends this war. We must speak out until we capture our own soul.

And I pledge to you—whatever my fate in the weeks ahead—that I will be with you. I will join with you to help save this Country, to help save the lives of our men, and to turn our time away from death, back to the business of life. For that is true to the best within us—and that is what we must make real.

Suggested Readings

The material listed below will provide additional information about and elaboration of the principles discussed in this book. Some works will primarily offer specific, practical advice for the speaker; others will introduce the student to more sophisticated concepts and models of criticism.

Books on the principles of public speaking

Andersen, Kenneth E. *Persuasion: Theory and Practice.* Boston: Allyn and Bacon, 1971.

Bettinghaus, Erwin P. *Persuasive Communication.* New York: Holt, Rinehart & Winston, 1968.

Blankenship, Jane. *Public Speaking: A Rhetorical Perspective.* Englewood Cliffs, N.J.: Prentice-Hall, 1969.

Borden, George A., Richard B. Gregg, and Theodore G. Grove. *Speech Behavior and Human Interaction.* Englewood Cliffs, N.J.: Prentice-Hall, 1969.

Brembeck, W. L., and W. S. Howell. *Persuasion.* Englewood Cliffs, N.J.: Prentice-Hall, 1952.

Buehler, E. C., and Wil A. Linkugel. *Speech Communication: A First Course.* New York: Harper & Row, 1969.

Cronkhite, Gary. *Persuasion: Speech and Behavioral Change.* Indianapolis, Ind.: Bobbs-Merrill, 1969.

Holtzman, Paul D. *The Psychology of Speakers' Audiences.* Glenview, Ill.: Scott, Foresman, 1970.

Howell, William S., and Ernest G. Bormann. *Presentational Speaking for Business and the Professions.* New York: Harper & Row, 1971.

Jeffrey, Robert C., and Owen Peterson. *Speech: A Text With Adapted Readings.* New York: Harper & Row, 1971.

Jensen, J. Vernon. *Perspectives on Oral Communication.* Boston: Holbrook, 1970.

King, Robert G. *Forms of Public Address.* Indianapolis, Ind.:
   Bobbs-Merrill, 1969.
Minnick, Wayne C. *The Art of Persuasion,* 2d. ed. Boston: Houghton
   Mifflin, 1968.
Mudd, Charles S., and Malcolm O. Sillers. *Speech: Content and
   Communication,* rev. ed. San Francisco: Chandler, 1969.
Murray, Elwood, Gerald M. Phillips, and J. David Truby. *Speech:
   Science-Art.* Indianapolis, Ind.: Bobbs-Merrill, 1969.
Nadeau, Ray E. *A Modern Rhetoric of Speech-Communication,* 2d
   ed. Reading, Mass.: Addison-Wesley, 1969.
Oliver, Robert T. *The Psychology of Persuasive Speech,* rev.
   impression. New York: McKay, 1968.
Oliver, Robert T., Harold P. Zelko, and Paul D. Holtzman. *Commun-
   icative Speaking and Listening,* 4th ed. New York: Holt,
   Rinehart & Winston, 1968.
Ross, Raymond. *Speech Communication: Fundamentals and
   Practice,* 2d ed. Englewood Cliffs, N.J.: Prentice-Hall, 1970.
Sarett, Alma Johnson, Lew Sarett, and William Trufant Foster. *Basic
   Principles of Speech,* 4th ed. Boston: Houghton Mifflin, 1966.
Smith, Raymond G. *Speech Communication: Theory and Models.*
   New York: Harper & Row, 1970.
Wilson, John F., and Carroll C. Arnold. *Public Speaking as a Liberal
   Art,* 2d ed. Boston: Allyn and Bacon, 1968.

Books on the criticism of public speaking

Auer, J. Jeffery (ed.). *The Rhetoric of Our Times.* New York:
   Appleton-Century-Crofts, 1969.
Bitzer, Lloyd. F., and Edwin Black (eds.). *The Prospect of Rhetoric:
   Report of the National Developmental Project.* Englewood
   Cliffs, N.J.: Prentice-Hall, 1971.
Black, Edwin B. *Rhetorical Criticism: A Study in Method.* New
   York: Macmillan, 1965.
Bormann, Ernest G. *Forerunners of Black Power: The Rhetoric of
   Abolition.* Englewood, Cliffs, N.J.: Prentice-Hall, 1971.
Bormann, Ernest G. *Theory and Research in the Communicative
   Arts.* New York: Holt, Rinehart & Winston, 1965.
Brandes, Paul D. *The Rhetoric of Revolt.* Englewood Cliffs, N.J.:
   Prentice-Hall, 1971.
Brockriede, Wayne, and Robert L. Scott. *Moments in the Rhetoric
   of the Cold War.* New York: Random House, 1970.

Cathcart, Robert, *Post Communication: Criticism and Evaluation.*
    Indianapolis, Ind.: Bobbs-Merrill, 1966.
Hillbruner, Anthony. *Critical Dimensions: The Art of Public Address
    Criticism.* New York: Random House, 1966.
Linsley, William A. (ed.), *Speech Criticism: Methods and Materials.*
    Dubuque, Iowa: William C. Brown, 1968.
Lomas, Charles W. *The Agitator in American Society.* Englewood
    Cliffs, N.J.: Prentice-Hall, 1968.
Nichols, Marie Hochmuth. *Rhetoric and Criticism.* Baton Rouge,
    La.: State University Press, 1963.
Nilsen, Thomas R. (ed.). *Essays on Rhetorical Criticism.* New York:
    Random House, 1968.
Quine, W. V., and J. S. Ullian. *The Web Belief.* New York: Random
    House, 1970.
Scott, Robert L., and Bernard L. Brock. *Methods of Rhetorical
    Criticism: A Twentieth Century Perspective.* New York: Harper
    & Row, 1972.
Scott, Robert L., and Wayne Brockriede. *The Rhetoric of Black
    Power.* New York: Harper & Row, 1969.
Smith, Arthur L. *The Rhetoric of Black Revolution.* Boston: Allyn
    and Bacon, 1969.
Smith, Arthur L., and Stephen Robb (eds.). *The Voice of Black
    Rhetoric.* Boston: Allyn and Bacon, 1971.
Thonssen, Lester, A. Craig Baird, and Waldo W. Braden. *Speech
    Criticism,* 2d ed. New York: Ronald, 1970.

Suggested Projects

The following projects are meant to suggest the kinds of exercises that might be undertaken to give the student critical experience. Each series of questions is not, of course, exhaustive, but is designed, rather, to point the direction that the critic might take.

General projects

1. Choose any of the critical introductions appearing in Chapters 3 through 8. Compare the chosen essay with the corresponding section in Chapter 2. In what ways does the author reflect the principle he has explained and discussed? Are there considerations he has not developed? Reexamine the speeches themselves. Is the emphasis of the critical essay justified by the speeches? In what ways are the conclusions reached in the essay supportable? Are there additional critical comments that the author might have made regarding the speeches under consideration? Would you have stated conclusions differently or reached additional conclusions?

2. Choose any speech presented and reexamine it in the light of principles not discussed in the critical introduction. For example, how does the Lincoln speech or the King speech promote identification between the audience and the topic and the audience and the speaker? To what extent and in what ways are these "reasonable" speeches? Does the pattern of the speech promote the speaker's goal and is it consistent with the needs of the occasion and the audience? How has language been used to reinforce the speaker's purpose? Would such an examination of all these factors cause you to question conclusions or judgments reached in the critical essay?

The primacy of the audience

3. Attend a public meeting at which there is a principal speaker. Prepare a profile of the audience including all you can observe

and discover about who the audience members are, why they are gathered together, their feelings toward the speaker and his position, and their expectations. Find as many specific examples as you can from the speech that demonstrate the ways in which the speaker did or did not take into account the salient audience characteristics that you have identified. Given the evidence you have gathered and the analysis you have performed, how well would you say that the speaker adapted to his specific audience?

4. Watch a nationally televised speech. From news reports and analyses, identify the varying audiences that might have been expected to view the speech. What in the speech indicates the speaker's awareness of different audiences? Does the speech itself suggest that the speaker was aware of audiences you had not considered? How would you account for the ways that the speaker approached different audiences—for example, does the speech suggest that some audiences may be more important to the speaker than others? Does the speaker attempt to reconcile conflicting goals or beliefs that might exist in different audiences?

Identification: The audience and the topic

5. Select a speech on a contemporary issue in which you are interested. (*Vital Speeches,* or *The New York Times*, or *The Congressional Digest* would be good sources of speeches.) Examine the speech carefully to discover the evidence of the speaker's values; do you find the speech persuasive to the extent that you share values with the speaker? Can you hypothesize the kinds of audiences who would find such values attractive and those who would find them unappealing? Are there conflicting values in the speech? If so, how does the speaker appear to reconcile them? In what ways and to what extent does the speaker attempt to involve the emotions of his listeners? For example, does the topic appear to be related to their feelings for others, their need to maintain their own health and safety, their desire for recognition, their collective and personal hopes and fears? Has the speaker exploited the audience's feelings skillfully? Can you suggest how the speaker might have made the topic more meaningful to the audience? Are there any extrinsic factors (e.g., ethical, political) that may account for the speaker's choices? To what extent did the speaker realize the possibilities of identification between the audience and the topic?

Identification: The audience and the speaker

6. Choose two speeches, one given by a prominent political, social, or religious figure, and one given by a student in a public speaking class. Compare and contrast the assets and liabilities that the speakers bring to each situation. What advantages and disadvantages does having a reputation known to the audience afford the speaker? How does each speaker deal with what is or is not known about his past positions, experiences, knowledge, and character? What evidence in the speech demonstrates the speaker's awareness of the nature and extent of his ethos? In what ways does each speaker appear to be enhancing or creating ethos? Are there examples in the speeches of actions that might tend to affect the speakers' ethos negatively? How well would you say each speaker dealt with the problem of ethos?

The quality of reasonableness

7. Select a speech from the past given on an issue you believe to be important. From historical material, reconstruct the setting in which the speech was given, paying particular attention to the audience values and assumptions contemporary to the speech. Through a careful examination of the speech, isolate the principal assumptions upon which the speaker's argument is based. Which of these seem to be in obvious accord with those held by the audience; which seem to be acceptable but in need of support to make them convincing to the audience? Do any of the speaker's assumptions seem to be in direct conflict with the audience's values and assumptions? In each case, how does the speaker present evidence to deal with the situation? What is the nature and extent of the evidence? In general, are the conclusions reached and generalizations made by the speaker warranted by the supporting material offered? To what extent does the speaker's strategy demonstrate his awareness of when, how much, and what kind of evidence was necessary for the audience he addressed?

The pattern of a speech

8. Listen to a speech given in a public speaking class. Can you identify the speaker's purpose? (In this situation you will have the opportunity to verify this with the speaker.) What were the speaker's important ideas? Do they grow clearly out of the specific purpose of the speech? Are the main ideas consistent

with each other? What discernible pattern do they follow? To what extent does the pattern seem to reflect audience imperatives? Does the topic itself suggest a certain pattern or impose limitations on the way the material is organized? Are there other organizational strategies the speaker might have employed, and how might these have improved upon the chosen pattern? In what ways is the evidence in the speech introduced at a place most calculated to promote understanding and make ideas more believable and acceptable? If a copy of the speaker's outline is available, examine it carefully to find and describe examples of the ways in which the speaker's planning demonstrated his organizational skills.

The style of a speech

9. Choose a recent Inaugural Address of a President of the United States. Examine carefully the language chosen and the constructions employed. In what ways might language choice be considered unusual by an audience? Would such choices tend to make the ideas under consideration more striking or challenging? Would they tend to make the ideas more clear? In what ways does the choice of language suggest the speaker's values or ways of looking at the world? Is there evidence in the speech to suggest that stylistic choices may have been made in order to provoke strong emotive responses on the part of the audience? How do the speaker's constructions imply contrasting or comparable values and ideas? To what extent do stylistic choices seem to govern or at least influence the organizational structure of the speech? Are there instances in which the speaker's language seems to supplement or substitute for evidence? In what ways is language choice designed to promote identification between the speaker and the audience?

Index